A Party Fit for Heroes

His Majesty's Garden Party for recipients of the Victoria Cross

26th June 1920

Derek Hunt and John Mulholland

With a Foreword by
Bill Speakman VC

First published in Great Britain, 2007 by
The Naval and Military Press Ltd
Unit 10, Ridgewood Industrial Park
Uckfield, East Sussex TN22 5QE
England
www.naval-military-press.com

British Library Cataloguing - in - Publication Data

A catalogue record for this book is available from the British Library

ISBN 1-847347-12-6

Front cover photograph :   King George V begins the inspection of the VCs on the lawn of
Buckingham Palace
(The Royal Collection,© 2007 Her Majesty Queen Elizabeth II)

Printed and bound in Great Britain by CPI Antony Rowe, Eastbourne

Contents

Illustrations

Abbreviations

ADC	Aide-de-Camp
AFC	Air Force Cross
AIF	Australian Imperial Force
Bt.	Baronet
CB	Companion of the Order of the Bath
CBE	Commander of the Order of the British Empire
CEF	Canadian Expeditionary Force
CMG	Companion of the Order of St Michael and St George
CO	Commanding Officer
CSM	Company Sergeant Major
DCLI	Duke of Cornwall's Light Infantry
DCM	Distinguished Conduct Medal
DLI	Durham Light Infantry
DSC	Distinguished Service Cross
DSM	Distinguished Service Medal
DSO	Distinguished Services Order
GC	George Cross
GCB	Knight Grand Cross of the Order of the Bath
GCSI	Knight Grand Commander of the Order of the Star of India
GCVO	Knight Grand Cross of the Royal Victorian Order
HAC	Honourable Artillery Company
HLI	Highland Light Infantry
HM	His/Her Majesty
HRH	His/Her Royal Highness
HQ	Headquarters
ISO	Imperial Service Order
IWM	Imperial War Museum
KCB	Knight Commander of the Order of the Bath
KCMG	Knight Commander of the Order of St Michael and St George
KCVO	Knight Commander of the Royal Victorian Order
KOYLI	King's Own Yorkshire Light Infantry
KOSB	King's Own Scottish Borderers
KRRC	King's Royal Rifle Corps
LG	The London Gazette
MBE	Member of the Order of the British Empire
MC	Military Cross
MM	Military Medal
MP	Member of Parliament
OBE	Officer of the Order of the British Empire
OM	Order of Merit
RA	Royal Artillery
RACD	Royal Army Chaplain's Department
RAF	Royal Air Force
RAMC	Royal Army Medical Corps
RASC	Royal Army Service Corps
RE	Royal Engineers
RFA	Royal Field Artillery
RFC	Royal Flying Corps
RGA	Royal Garrison Artillery
RHA	Royal Horse Artillery
RHQ	Regimental Headquarters
RMA	Royal Marine Artillery
RMLI	Royal Marine Light Infantry
RN	Royal Navy
RNR	Royal Navy Reserve
RNVR	Royal Naval Volunteer Reserve
VC	Victoria Cross

**1. Private Bill Speakman VC after the presentation of his
VC ribbon in Japan, December 1951**
(Photograph courtesy of the Imperial War Museum, London KOR/U5)

**2. Bill Speakman VC on 20 May 2003 at the unveiling of the plaque of
'Speakman's Bridge' in his home town of Altrincham** *(John Mulholland)*

Foreword
by
Bill Speakman VC

It is an honour and a privilege to be invited to write a foreword to this extraordinary book.

The Royal Garden Party of 26 June 1920 was a unique occasion: it was the first official reunion of VC recipients since the founding of the decoration in 1856. The VCs who attended represented conflicts from the Indian Mutiny in 1857 to the campaign in North Russia in 1919.

The event was not an entirely private occasion as the public had the opportunity to watch the VCs march from Wellington Barracks to Buckingham Palace. I could identify with Gordon Campbell VC who recorded that he felt ill-at-ease during the march as he thought of the thousands of others who had earned the VC but whose acts remained unrecognised.

Over the last 50 years I have had the honour of meeting many VC holders particularly at the biennial reunions organised by the Victoria Cross and George Cross Association. At the VC Centenary celebrations in 1956 I remember meeting VCs who had been present at the Garden Party. They spoke of the occasion with fond memories as we walked across the parade ground at Wellington Barracks where they had assembled in 1920 for the march to the Palace.

When the VC was instituted, Queen Victoria was insistent that anyone in her armed forces was eligible for the award irrespective of rank, status, age, race or religion. In one sense it was a paradox: the VC was inclusive in that anyone was eligible but exclusive in that few were awarded. Queen Victoria required a democratic award and it was a radical idea at the time. This underlying democratic value has never been lost and was evident at the Garden Party in 1920. As this book describes, it surprised many present - not least the VCs themselves. I expect Queen Victoria would have been pleased.

The authors are to be congratulated in bringing to light this long-forgotten event. The Party was held during a turbulent period and the controversial issues of the day are not avoided. The description of the event and the human details are enhanced by the memories of those who were there.

This year marks the 150th anniversary of the first VC Investiture and therefore this book comes at an appropriate time to record one of the grandest occasions in the history of the decoration.

Bill Speakman VC

Acknowledgements

We are grateful to The Royal Collection, Windsor Castle for permission to reproduce extracts from the diaries of King George V and Queen Mary, which are copyright of Her Majesty Queen Elizabeth II. The Royal Collection also kindly permitted us to reproduce several photographs from Queen Mary's album, which are also copyright of Her Majesty Queen Elizabeth II.

We would like to thank Mrs Carol Scott, a grand-daughter of Oliver Brooks VC, who provided a starting point for the book by supplying various documents sent to VC recipients before the Garden Party.

The staff of the following institutions have been of great assistance and many of them have allowed us to reproduce material from their archives, for which we are grateful: The National Army Museum for access to the Canon Lummis VC files (held on behalf of the Military Historical Society), The British Library Newspaper Library, Slough Library, The Royal Artillery Museum and the Dingwall Museum Trust.

We should like to thank The Imperial War Museum, The Illustrated London News Picture Library, The Daily Mirror, Jarrolds Publishing, Andrew Lawson, Glendinning's, Dingwall Museum Trust, Aerofilms, Falcon Crest and Dix Noonan Webb for permission to reproduce photographs for which they own the copyright.

Whilst every effort has been made to trace the copyright holders or the photographers of illustrations used this has not always proved possible. Should anyone feel that a photograph has been used without proper accreditation please contact the publisher.

Many individuals have helped us and we would particularly like to thank David Erskine-Hill, Christopher Hunt, Tom Johnson, Alan Jordan and Steve Snelling.

Our thanks are due to Gail Balfour, Barbara Hunt and Rebecca Lee for producing many drafts of the manuscript.

Finally, we are deeply indebted to Bill Speakman VC for writing the Foreword.

Preface

The first gathering of Victoria Cross recipients took place on 26 June 1857 when Queen Victoria personally decorated 62 recipients at the first investiture in Hyde Park. The 1920 Garden Party was the first VC reunion and the largest official gathering of VCs since 1857.

The Garden Party of 1920 has been largely forgotten and was perhaps eclipsed on 9 November 1929 when HRH The Prince of Wales hosted the famous VC Dinner at the House of Lords. The only event to match any of these reunions was the 1956 VC Centenary celebrations in London, which culminated in the VC ceremony and march past on 26 June in Hyde Park before HM The Queen. Although it was 99 years since Queen Victoria first decorated her subjects, it was 100 years since the Royal Warrant which founded the decoration.

However, the 1920 Garden Party was far from being low key; it was given much coverage in the newspapers and magazines of the day. It was held within two years of the end of the Great War and the ranks of VC holders were swelled by that conflict. Three out of every four VCs present at the Garden Party had received their award for the Great War.

In 1920 Britain and its Empire, although victors with their Allies, were still coming to terms with the impact of the Great War and the loss of a generation of young men. The mood of the nation was one of grief and there was financial hardship for many. In this context some sort of ostentatious display might have been inappropriate. The 1920 Garden Party brought together veterans from distant campaigns including the Indian Mutiny, Afghanistan, Zulu and Boer Wars. In an oddly British way, the event was organised in a hurry, but nevertheless efficiently, and even the threatening summer rain did not spoil the occasion. Many who were present remarked on the friendliness and informality of the event. In his diary King George V called it "a great success".

It was a grand occasion but rarely merits a footnote, even in books solely about the Victoria Cross. It is, therefore, with much pleasure that we bring this event to light and hope this publication will act as a memorial to the VC recipients present on that occasion and record an important milestone in the history of the Victoria Cross.

Derek Hunt and John Mulholland

26 June 2007

1 A Short History of the Victoria Cross

The Victoria Cross was founded by Royal Warrant on 29 January 1856 to be awarded to officers and other ranks of the Navy and Army, who, serving in the presence of an enemy, should have "performed some signal act of valour or devotion to their country."

Queen Victoria was moved to introduce a decoration which was exclusively for acts of valour and to be differentiated from existing honours and awards. It was democratic in the sense that any rank could win the decoration and that it needed to be unquestionably earned.

Since its institution a total of 1,356 VCs have been awarded, including second award bars to three army officers. After the First World War an award was made to the American Unknown Soldier buried at Arlington Cemetery, Virginia near Washington DC.

The first announcement of recipients appeared in *The London Gazette* on 24 February 1857, for services in the Baltic and Crimea. The Queen personally decorated 62 VC recipients at the first investiture at Hyde Park on 26 June 1857. Some of these awards were made retrospectively to dates before the date of the VC Warrant. For example, the first winner of the VC was Charles Lucas, a 20 year old Mate of HMS *Hecla*, who, on 21 June 1854, threw a live shell from the deck of his ship. He was immediately promoted to Lieutenant and retired with the rank of Rear-Admiral. Lucas was amongst those decorated at the first investiture.

3. Example of a Victoria Cross *(Glendinning's)*

The reverse side of the VC worn by A.H. Proctor at the 1920 VC Garden Party. As a stretcher bearer in the King's (Liverpool) Regiment he tended two wounded men in no-man's land on 4 June 1916. Proctor later became an Anglican clergyman and served as an RAF chaplain in the Second World War. He died in 1973.

Over the years a number of Royal Warrants have been introduced or changes made to existing Warrants. For instance, King George V felt strongly that the VC should never be forfeited and in 1920 this clause was introduced. Prior to that date a total of eight VCs had been forfeited for a variety of offences. Also, in 1902, King Edward VII introduced the principle of awarding VCs posthumously and in 1911 native officers and men of the Indian Army became eligible.

Since its institution the VC has been manufactured by the London jewellers Hancocks and Co, who were established in 1849. The design of the VC was selected by Queen Victoria as a simple Maltese Cross of bronze cast from Chinese cannons captured from the Russians at Sebastopol.

On the upper arm is a lion above a crown under which are the words 'For Valour.' The name, rank and unit of the recipient is engraved on the rear of the suspended bar and the date of the VC action at the centre of the reverse side of the cross.

The VC is worn suspended by a red ribbon 1½" wide. Originally there was a blue ribbon for the Navy and red for the Army. In 1920 a Royal Warrant standardised this to a red ribbon for all services including the Royal Air Force. When the ribbon only is worn, a miniature replica of the Cross is borne on its centre. This is to distinguish the VC ribbon from similar looking ribbons such as the Order of the Bath.

When the VC was first instituted a pension of £10 per year was payable to non-commissioned holders. In 1898 it was decided this amount might be increased to £50 in times of need and later to £75. In 1959 all ranks became eligible and the sum was increased to £100 with a further increase in 1995 to £1,300. It now stands at £1,450.

When Queen Victoria instituted the VC she intended it "to be highly prized and eagerly sought after by the Officers and Men of Our Naval and Military Services." A retrospective view shows that her original intention has been fulfilled.

CSM William John George Evans VC

CSM Evans, of 18th Battalion The Manchester Regiment, gained his VC during the attack on Guillemont, France on 30 July 1916. While under heavy rifle and machine gun fire he volunteered to carry an important message after five runners had been killed attempting to do so. He succeeded in delivering the message and although wounded, undertook the hazardous return journey. Shortly after re-joining his company he was captured by the enemy and spent the next two years as a prisoner-of-war. He was exchanged into neutral Holland in June 1918 and returned to England in November 1918

It is most likely that those who recommended Evans for the VC were also taken prisoner, and it was not until they had been released after the war that the recommendation could be made through the usual channels. The VC citation appeared in *The London Gazette* on 30 January 1920. Evans was invested with the VC at Buckingham Palace on 12 March 1920 - the last VC awarded of the Great War and the last investiture before the Garden Party. Evans died in September 1937, aged 61.

2 1920 - A Year of Turmoil

The year of 1920 marked the beginning of a decade of social and political unrest in both Britain and mainland Europe. Britain and her Allies were recovering from the aftermath of the Great War and the political maps of Europe and the Middle East were being redrawn. In January 1920 the League of Nations was founded and although the Treaty of Versailles was signed in June 1919, negotiations regarding German reparation payments continued into 1920. A conference took place in Spa, Belgium in July 1920, attended by the British Prime Minister, David Lloyd George, and German delegates.

In the wake of the Great War most of Europe's monarchies had been swept away. In 1917 King George V had distanced the Royal Family from its German ancestry by changing the family name from Saxe-Coburg-Gotha to Windsor. In the midst of the social unrest of 1920, despite some anti-royalist feelings, the King and the Royal Family enjoyed a large measure of respect and popularity.

Further afield the Bolsheviks were exerting their grip on Russia, and the Greeks were on the offensive in Asia Minor against Turkish nationalists. In the USA prohibition had begun. On 28 April in San Remo the British mandate to control Palestine and Mesopotamia was confirmed by the League of Nations. Britain was given a new Middle Eastern domain from the debris of the Turkish Empire. In the newly formed Iraq British troops were active in suppressing the Arab insurrection. Three posthumous VCs were announced in 1920 but none was gazetted by the time of the Garden Party.

Closer to home the troubles in Ireland continued. Throughout 1920 violence flared and a number of political assassinations occurred. The Royal Irish Constabulary enrolled its first British special constables who were distinguished by their black and tan uniforms. In December 1920 the King signed an Act of Parliament which partitioned Ireland into two and after years of escalating violence the Irish Free State was finally established two years later.

In June athletes were training for the Olympic Games. The British athlete Albert Hill was not disappointed: he took two gold medals at Antwerp in August. Lieutenant Harry Daniels VC MC, who attended the Garden Party, represented Britain in the boxing team.

Strikes became ever more common as the post-war economic depression tightened its grip; a total of two million workers were involved in strikes during the year and 27 million working days were lost. Although the majority of those on strike had genuine grievances and a desire for a decent standard of living, many strikes were politically motivated. In July the Communist Party of Great Britain was formed.

Some notable developments occurred in the world of entertainment during the year. Jazz, a new form of music, was catching on. It had been introduced during the First World War by US servicemen. During 1920 the British Board of Film Censors was established and Marconi opened the first public broadcasting station. The day before the Garden Party it was announced that The Hague was to be seat of the International Court of Justice, as it still is today. On the day of the Garden Party, Lord French, the former Commander-in-Chief of the British Expeditionary Force, was visiting Belfast to unveil a memorial window to the Ulster Division. This ceremony was not

3

without risks as the previous December the IRA had tried to assassinate Lord French in his position as the Lord Lieutenant of Ireland.

A "Warrant Effecting a General Revision and Recodification of the Conditions of Award of the Victoria Cross" was issued on 22 May 1920. This consolidated the original warrant of 1856 and all subsequent warrants. It was the first new warrant since the formation of the RAF, which was included in the list of eligibility. "Matrons, sisters, nurses and staff of the nursing services" were also made eligible for the decoration, although no woman has yet been awarded the VC. The opportunity was also taken in the new warrant to standardise the colour of the VC ribbon.

4. Unveiling of the Cenotaph, Whitehall, 11 November 1920
(Photograph courtesy of the Imperial War Museum, London. Q31488)

"On the stroke of eleven, the King pressed a knob on the top of a little pedestal erected in the road, and the two great Union Jacks that draped the Cenotaph fell to the ground. At the same moment the King raised his cap. Bareheaded and silent, he stood in the midst of this vast gathering of silent people. At the end of the Two Minutes, the band struck up and the choir led the singing of 'O God, our help in ages past' while the drums, draped in black, rolled low thunder in the intervals."
(The Daily Herald, 12 November 1920)

1920 brought a number of tributes to the war heroes of Britain and the Empire. On 9 June King George V opened the Imperial War Museum which was then housed at the Crystal Palace. Also, a permanent Cenotaph was built in Whitehall to honour the dead of the Great War. This was unveiled on 11 November 1920 on the second anniversary of the Armistice and on the same day an Unknown Warrior was buried with full military honours in Westminster Abbey. Out of the

100 decorated men forming the Guard of Honour 74 were recipients of the VC, many of whom five months earlier were themselves being honoured at the Garden Party.

On the afternoon of the Garden Party crowds flocked to see the VCs marching to the Palace but there were other celebrities at large in London: the actress Mary Pickford and her new husband, Douglas Fairbanks, who were spending the weekend at the home of the Duke and Duchess of Sutherland. The *Sunday Express* correspondent was in no doubt about which was the most significant spectacle:

> Those Londoners who, exhausted by their chase after Mary Pickford, failed to turn up in Green Park and swell the modest attendance into a multitude missed a sight which they may never see again - the most inspiring sight that London has witnessed in my lifetime.

3 Preparations

By the time the first VC reunion was held in June 1920, the Victoria Cross had been awarded 1,155 times. The last man to be gazetted was Company Sergeant Major George Evans, whose VC for bravery during the Somme offensive in 1916 had not been announced in *The London Gazette* until 30 January 1920 (see box on page 2).

Over half the VCs awarded between 1856 and 1920 were for the Great War. Between 1914 and 1919 a total of 632 VCs were awarded, including two bars. Over 30 percent of the Great War awards were posthumous.

To honour the surviving VCs of all conflicts King George V decided to hold a reunion. It was thought that the garden of Buckingham Palace would be an appropriate venue and this would provide an informal setting for recipients to bring relatives and even some of their children. Although the public were to be excluded they would have the opportunity to see the heroes as they marched from Wellington Barracks to the Palace via The Mall.

Invitations to the Garden Party were sent to all VC recipients on behalf of the King by the War Office. Former Sergeant Oliver Brooks VC received his reply-paid telegram, via RHQ Coldstream Guards, at his home in Alexandra Road, Windsor.

The telegram, dated 7 June 1920, read:

> The King giving afternoon party to all recipients Victoria Cross accompanied by two relations on 26th. Wire immediately if will attend and names and relationships of those coming. Travelling warrants will be provided.

Sergeant Oliver Brooks VC

Lance-Sergeant Oliver Brooks, of 3rd Battalion Coldstream Guards, was awarded the VC for leading a bombing party which recaptured 200 yards of trench near Loos, on 8 October 1915. He was promoted to sergeant the following day.

He is, perhaps, better known as the only man to receive his VC at the Sovereign's bedside. This unique form of investiture was the result of a serious fall from a horse by King George V, who was reviewing troops in France. The horse was frightened by sudden cheering and reared up, dismounted the King and landed on him. The King suffered severe injuries, including a fractured pelvis. Although in great pain, the King wished to proceed as planned with personally decorating Brooks with the VC.

Brooks was brought to the King's hospital train on 1 November 1915 and knelt at his bedside, where a private ceremony took place. The King was not strong enough to get the VC pin through the thick khaki of Brooks's tunic and had to be assisted before the investiture could be completed.

After the Great War Brooks settled in Windsor where he became a hotel commissionaire. He died in October 1940, aged 51.

Brooks replied to say that he would be attending and would be accompanied by his wife. When those invited had responded, lists were drawn up of those who could probably attend and those who were unlikely to be present. Official invitation cards were sent to those VCs who confirmed they would attend.

As with the first VC investiture of 1857, this was a hurriedly organised event. The invitations were issued less than three weeks before the occasion and this partially explains why the attendance rate was to be relatively low. A number of VC recipients lived overseas, and even with longer notice they would probably still have been unable to attend. Many VCs had remained in the forces after the Great War and some were on active duty at the time of the Garden Party.

The choice of the date of 26 June was significant.[1] This was the same date chosen by Queen Victoria for the first investiture in 1857. The tradition continued for the VC centenary celebrations when HM Queen Elizabeth II inspected VC holders at Hyde Park on 26 June 1956. On 26 June 2006 a Service of Commemoration was held at Westminster Abbey to mark the 150th anniversary of the Institution of the VC and the 50th anniversary of the founding of the VC and GC Association.

Buckingham Palace was an appropriate venue and in keeping with tradition. The Palace had been the official London residence of the Sovereign since the beginning of Queen Victoria's reign in 1837. Many of the VC recipients had been decorated at the Palace during the First World War. Although the VCs and guests were not to be admitted to the State Rooms, the garden where the gathering was to be held was magnificent - particularly at that time of year.

Railway warrants for the train journey to and from London were sent to VCs and their guests on 19 June. Colonel H.C. Sutton, Administration, HQ London District, was responsible for issuing warrants and ensuring the travel arrangements ran smoothly.

For those VC recipients who had long journeys and were unable to return home that night, certain allowances were payable, the amount depending on rank and whether still serving in the forces. Allowances were issued, against a completed application form, at Wellington Barracks between 2.00 and 2.30 pm on the day of the Garden Party.

The Times recorded that invitations were issued to some relatives of deceased VCs. For example, the fiancée of Pte. J. Lynn VC DCM was invited. However, it is known that the widow of Brigadier-General P. A. Kenna VC DSO ADC was not invited. Kenna had been an ADC to King George V before the First World War and was killed at Gallipoli. So the criteria for inviting the relatives of deceased VCs were unclear.

The VCs were restricted to each bringing two relatives. However, some flexibility was shown by the authorities. For example, *The Daily Mail* recorded that Sergeant Welch VC (The Royal Berkshire Regiment) brought his wife and two babies. Sergeant Welch explained to the authorities that unless he brought both his children, his wife would not be able to attend. So an extra ticket was granted.

---

[1] 26 June was a significant date for Charles Ward who was awarded the VC for action at Lindley, South Africa on 26 June 1900. So the Garden Party coincided with the 20th anniversary of the action. Ward, who was present at the Garden Party, was the last VC to be personally decorated by Queen Victoria, on 15 December 1900.

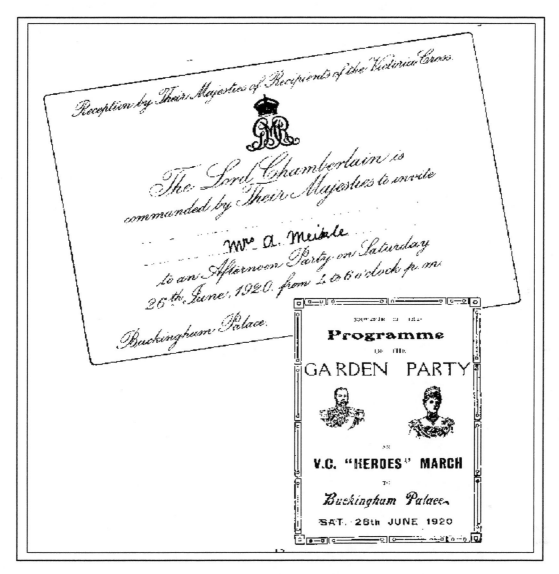

5. Invitation Card and unofficial Souvenir Programme (*Dingwall Museum Trust*)

The Times recorded that invitations were issued to some relatives of deceased VCs. An example is shown here to Mrs A. Meikle, the mother of Sergeant M. J. Meikle VC MM of the Seaforth Highlanders. Also shown is an unofficial programme which was distributed on the day to relatives of the VCs and the crowds lining the march route.

In 1920 Britain was in an economic depression following the rapid change from war-time full production and the addition of over four million demobilized servicemen into the labour market. Between 1914 and 1920 prices had risen by 250% but wages had failed to match these increases. As a result for many people, VCs included, there was very little to live on.

The Daily Herald[2], one of the more militant newspapers of the time, interviewed the General Secretary of the National Federation of Discharged Soldiers and Sailors on 25 June.

---

[2] *The Daily Herald* started publication in 1910 as a newssheet for strikers and considered itself the organ of the Labour Movement. It ceased publication in September 1964.

He had been able to supply half-a-dozen VC recipients with suits for the occasion. "And", he continued, "there are many men who, though their suits may be fairly decent, will have had to buy new collars and ties and little extras of that kind in order to look smart for the occasion... quite a number of them will have gone without their dinners during the past few days to make themselves presentable".

In a more uncompromising theme *The Daily Herald* also reported that several London VCs were members of the National Union of Ex-Servicemen. "Three men", reported the Union Secretary, "will not attend the royal tea-fight. They are too busy attacking the system of which the King is the figurehead. They accepted the King's invitation once before, and they are not going to accept another, whether it is a blood-fight or a tea-fight".

The identity of these three VCs is uncertain but it indicates some of the feelings which were current in the aftermath of the Great War. This story was reported elsewhere, including an Australian newspaper which concluded that several men declined the King's invitation to the Garden Party because they were too poor to obtain decent clothes. They had been advised to go, it was reported, so that they might show the public their hardship. In contrast, the Admiralty had instructed naval officer VC recipients to wear number four frockcoat with sword.

The Daily Mirror, however, played down any class differences and social unrest:

> Advantages of wealth and social distinction will be lost on this occasion. The one peer in the procession, Viscount Gort, will, according to the official list, have as his nearest neighbour Lance Corporal W.D. Fuller, from his own regiment, the Grenadier Guards.

6. Two Grenadier Guards VCs *(Illustrated Sunday Herald)*

Major Viscount Gort VC DSO** MVO MC (left) with Lance-Corporal W. D. Fuller VC, both of the Grenadier Guards. Gort was later the Commander-in-Chief of the British Expeditionary Force during the fall of France and the evacuation from Dunkirk in 1940. His son-in-law, Major W. P. Sidney, Lord De L'Isle, won a VC at Anzio in 1944. Fuller can be seen wearing the VC, 1914/15 Star and the Cross of St. George 3rd class (Russia) presented to him by King George V on 29 September 1915.

10

A similar report was filed by the *Evening Standard* whose reporter wrote:

> Most of the men with whom I talked had got into quite satisfactory employment in civilian life. One or two were employed by the Government and some had come back into office life. Some had gone into the workshop, and some onto the farm; but amongst them all I did not hear a single note of discontent or dissatisfaction.

7. Invitation Card to the Garden Party *(Photograph courtesy of the Imperial War Museum, London)*

The front and reverse of invitation card to S. J. Bent VC MM covered with signatures he collected on the day. On the front of the invitation card at bottom centre Bent put his own signature as "S J Bent VC MM". Just above his signature is that of E. H. Pitcher VC and to the right of Sgt Jack Ripley VC who added "1st Black Watch 26-6-20". Both Pitcher and Ripley appear in photograph 8. Beneath Ripley's signature is the inverted signature of Theodore Veale VC (see Chapter 10). In the top right hand corner is the signature of the widow of Pte Walter Mills VC who died of gas poisoning during his VC action at Givenchy, France on 11 December 1917.

CSM Spencer John Bent VC MM

Spencer John Bent, better known as 'Joe' Bent, enlisted as a drummer boy in the 1st Battalion East Lancashire Regiment in 1905. In 1914 the battalion took part in the First Battle of Ypres, where Bent earned his VC.

On the night of 1-2 November 1914, while near Le Gheer in Belgium, he took command of his unit when his officers had been struck down. He held the position and successfully fought off a German attack the next morning.

On 3 November Bent rescued Private McNulty, who was lying wounded on the ground in front of the British trenches. When he reached the wounded private, Bent was unable to stand up to carry him back without attracting enemy fire. He slipped his legs under McNulty's arms and, using his elbows, dragged him back to their trench.

A week later Bent was seriously wounded in his right leg and sent to hospital in England for treatment. By the end of the War he had reached the rank of CSM and had also won the MM.

After leaving the army he became a school janitor and during the Second World War rejoined his old regiment. Joe Bent died, aged 86, in May 1977.

4 Lunch at Wellington Barracks

Many of the VCs and their relatives travelled to London by train on the morning of 26 June. Some travelled on overnight trains from Scotland and from other distant locations. Others travelled up the day before. The special day began at 12.30 pm at Wellington Barracks, where the officers of the Brigade of Guards entertained the VCs and their relatives to lunch. The Barracks are located at the western end of Birdcage Walk just 200 yards from the Palace.

Lunch was served in a large marquée in the barracks square while thousands of spectators clambered around the railings and young Guardsmen gathered near the barracks to witness the unique occasion. Some of the VC holders wore uniforms but many were in civilian dress, some in morning coats and top hats; others wore bowlers, straw hats or caps.

Captain J. G. Smyth VC (later Brigadier Sir John Smyth VC) recalled in his autobiography:[3]

> On 26 June 1920 I attended the first Victoria Cross Reunion, a very momentous and moving occasion, which was attended by great crowds. The Garden Party at Buckingham Palace was preceded by a luncheon at Wellington Barracks where the band of the Welsh Guards played throughout the meal...

Corporal Veale VC kept a diary of the day (see Chapter 10) and recorded:

8. Army and naval VCs at Wellington Barracks *(Illustrated Sunday Herald)*

Left to right Sgt. J. Ripley VC and Petty Officer E. Pitcher VC DSM RN
flanked by two Chelsea pensioners in front of the marquée.

---

[3] *Milestones*, Sidgwick and Jackson, 1979.

At Wellington Barracks, where we assembled, I met Major Fosse VC, of my old brigade, and he introduced me to the different staff officers. I got autographs from General Murlin VC[4], Commander Holbrook VC, Colonel Sherwood Kelly VC - in fact, I obtained about 150. The refreshments there were laid out in real Army style, with red, white and blue flowers on the tables. The officer, who spoke on behalf of the Brigade of Guards, said it was a most rushed affair, and they had tried to do their best. But there was really everything we wanted there.

It is unclear how many people attended the lunch at Wellington Barracks. The invitation to lunch came with the letter dated 19 June from Colonel Sutton enclosing the joining instructions and travel warrants. In his letter he asked the VCs to let him know if they intended to accept the lunch invitation. Even if this request was responded to immediately, the Guards would have had very little notice of the numbers attending. So the planning of the lunch was rushed, as was the lunch itself. The confusion is reflected in the timing of the lunch. The invitation stated lunch was at 12.30 pm but the 'Summary of Procedure' stated 1.00 pm.

9. An autograph-collecting VC *(Illustrated Sunday Herald)*

Sgt Issy Smith VC collects the autograph of Colonel E. D. Brown-Synge-Hutchinson VC CB at Wellington Barracks before the march. See photograph 44.

---

[4] No person named Murlin was awarded the VC. Veale may have meant Colonel Sir Percival Marling VC CB and was confused about his rank.

Another purpose for gathering the VCs at Wellington Barracks before the march was to issue their travel and accommodation allowances. The instructions sent out were addressed to both VC recipients and to some of the next of kin of deceased VCs. This confirms the fact that deceased VCs were not forgotten and some of their relatives did attend the event. These expenses were to be paid between 2.00 pm and 2.30 pm. Also, those who had ordered free tickets for the Alhambra theatre performance collected them at the same time. Sir Oswald Stoll had donated 300 seats to the VCs and their relatives for the evening performance of *Johnny Jones, a Robey Salad*. A member of the staff of the Alhambra was present to distribute the tickets.

10. Five naval VCs at Wellington Barracks before the march
(Photograph courtesy of the Imperial War Museum. London. Q66160)

The naval VCs from left to right are Lieutenant P. Dean VC, Lieutenant G. Steele VC, Lieutenant A. Agar VC DSO, Admiral of the Fleet Sir Arthur Wilson VC and Captain E. Unwin VC CB CMG (see also photograph 14). The marquée in the background was used for lunch and behind is the Guards Chapel. This chapel was totally destroyed on 18 June 1944 by a V1 flying bomb which hit the building during a service and resulted in great loss of life. The chapel was rebuilt in the 1960s. The buildings in the background right were also destroyed and now form The Home Office which can be seen in photograph 29.

Agar and Unwin were still awaiting their medals for service in the First World War and wear the ribbons only. To the left of Dean in the background is General Sir Reginald Hart VC KCB KCVO who is wearing two Royal Humane Society Medals on his right breast. On the far right in the background is Lieutenant-Colonel Harry Greenwood VC DSO* MC.

To process all this paperwork and issue allowances and tickets in 30 minutes must have taken some organisation. It appears to have taken over an hour. During this period there was an informal reunion in the square where guests and friends renewed acquaintances. Photographers made the most of the occasion, quickly taking pictures as they had the opportunity. The VCs then went to find their place in the marching order while their relatives passed through the crowds and walked across the road to the Palace.

While the lunch was progressing at Wellington Barracks the King and Queen were lunching at the Palace with the Hon. Sir Thomas Mackenzie, who had been invested earlier in the day with the Knight Grand Cross of the Order of St Michael and St George. Sir Thomas held a number of positions in the government of New Zealand before becoming Prime Minister, for a brief period, in 1912. He was the High Commissioner for New Zealand from 1912 to 1920.

11. Captain. John Smyth VC MC
(Illustrated Sunday Herald)

Captain John Smyth VC MC with his mother and fiancée at Wellington Barracks.

Captain John George Smyth VC MC (Later Brigadier The Rt. Hon. Sir John Smyth Bt. VC MC MP)

John Smyth, then a lieutenant serving with the Indian Army, was awarded his VC for bravery on 18 May 1915 near Richebourg L' Avoue, France. With a small party of volunteers he successfully carried a supply of bombs to within 20 yards of the enemy's position, over exceptionally dangerous ground. Smyth was awarded his MC for gallantry in action in Waziristan on 22 October 1919. In the same action Captain H. J. Andrews of the Indian Medical Service was awarded a posthumous VC (LG 9 September 1920). Smyth also served during the Second World War. In 1950 he entered parliament as the Conservative member for Norwood and in 1956 was one of the founders of the Victoria Cross Association. He became its first Chairman, and succeeded Sir Winston Churchill as President in 1965. Sir 'Jackie' was a successful author and wrote nearly 30 books, including two volumes of autobiography and *The Story of the Victoria Cross 1856-1963*. He died in April 1983.

12. Three VCs at Wellington Barracks before the march
(Illustrated Sunday Herald)

Left to right, Pte. J. Osborne VC, Pte. T. Flawn VC and Lieutenant-Colonel J. Sherwood-Kelly VC CMG DSO. Wellington Barracks can be seen in the background and can be compared with a modern day view in the photograph below.

13. Modern day view of Wellington Barracks *(John Mulholland)*

5 March to the Palace

At about 2.45 pm the VCs were grouped by services and regiments in accordance with the list prepared for the march. Procedure notes had been sent to all VCs taking part explaining how the groups should be made up:

> The recipients will greatly assist if they will assemble facing the group numbers on the railings of Wellington Barracks, the first section of fours being 1 to 4, next 5 to 8 etc. Should any be unavoidably absent, it is proposed to leave a blank file.

14. Group No. 1 prepare for the march outside Wellington Barracks

Front row left to right: Admiral of the Fleet Sir Arthur Wilson VC GCB OM GCVO, Lieutenant-Colonel L. Halliday VC CB RMLI, Commander B. Guy VC DSO, Lieutenant-Commander N. Holbrook VC. In the second row Captains Ritchie and Nasmith are partially hidden. But clearly visible are Captain E. Unwin VC CB CMG and Petty Officer G. Samson VC (both smiling). In third row, two behind Wilson is Captain G. Campbell VC DSO and clearly visible is Petty Officer E. Pitcher VC DSM (bearded towards rear in fifth row). See also photograph 18.

All the VCs attending were given a copy of the marching order by group number and their position in each group. The official document issued by the War Office was eight pages long and is shown in Appendix 1. The first page of the actual list is shown on page 20. Some of the VCs can be seen holding their copies in the above photograph and in photograph 16.

HIS MAJESTY'S GARDEN PARTY TO RECIPIENTS

OF THE

VICTORIA CROSS, 26th JUNE, 1920.

List by Services and Regiments for march to Buckingham Palace.

GROUP No. 1.

1. Admiral of the Fleet Sir Arthur Knyvet Wilson, G.C.B., O.M., G.C.V.O., R.N.,
2. Lieutenant-Colonel Lewis Stratford Tollemache Halliday, C.B., R.M.L.I.,
3. Commander Basil John Douglas Guy, D.S.O., R.N.,
4. Lieutenant-Commander Norman Douglas Holbrook, R.N.,
5. Commander Henry Peel Ritchie, R.N.,
6. Captain Martin Eric Nasmith, C.B., R.N.,
7. Captain Edward Unwin, C.B., C.M.G., R.N.,
8. Petty Officer George McKenzie Samson, R.N.R.,
9. Commander Richard Bell Davies, D.S.O., A.F.C., R.N.,
10. Captain Hon. Edward Barry Stewart Bingham, O.B.E., R.N.,
11. Captain Gordon Campbell, D.S.O., R.N.,
12. Lance Corporal Walter Richard Parker, R.M.L.I.,
13. Lieutenant Ronald Neil Stuart, D.S.O., R.N.R.,
14. Leading Seaman William Williams, D.S.M., R.N.R.,
15. Chief Skipper Joseph Watt, R.N.R.,
16. Lieutenant Charles George Bonner, D.S.C., R.N.R.,
17. Petty Officer Ernest Pitcher, D.S.M., R.N.,
18. Captain Alfred Francis Blakeley Carpenter, R.N.,
19. Lieutenant Percy Thompson-Deane, R.N.V.R.,
20. Sergeant Norman Augustus Finch, R.M.A.,
21. Lieutenant-Commander Geoffrey Heneage Drummond, R.N.V.R.,
22. Lieutenant Harold Auten, D.S.C., R.N.R.,
23. Lieutenant Augustine Willington Shelton Agar, D.S.O., R.N.,
24. Lieutenant Gordon Charles Steele, RN.,

GROUP No. 2.

1. Private J. Duogan, 1st (King's) Dragoon Guards,
2. Major-General Sir N. M. Smyth, K.O.B., 2nd Dragoon Guards (Queen's Bays),
3. Sergeant H. Engleheart, 10th (Prince of Wales's Own Royal) Hussars,
4. Colonel E. D. Brown-Synge-Hutchinson, C.B., 14th (King's) Hussars,
5. Sergeant C. E. Garforth, 15th (The King's) Hussars
6. Private H. G. Crandon, 18th (Queen Mary's Own) Royal Hussars,
7. Private T. Byrne, 21st (Empress of India's) Lancers,
8. Shoeing Smith C. Hull, 21st (Empress of India's) Lancers,
9. Lance-Corporal F. W. O. Potts, Berks Yeomanry,
10. S.S. Corporal A. E. Ind, Royal Artillery,
11. Sergeant J. C. Raynes, Royal Artillery,

(22560-43)   500   6/20   H & S

15. Front page of the Official Marching Order
For full list see Appendix 1.

20

16. Group No. 4 prepare for the march outside Wellington Barracks
(Photograph courtesy of the Imperial War Museum, London. Q69203)

In the front row are left to right: Sergeant R. E. Elcock VC MM, Captain H. Reynolds VC MC and Private H. H. Robson VC, all of the Royal Scots (Lothian Regiment). These three VCs also feature in photograph 47. The fourth VC, with arms folded, is Brigadier-General W. D. Wright VC CMG DSO the Queen's (Royal West Surrey) Regiment. To the right and in the background are the drums and members of the Welsh Guards band. In row two and hidden by Elcock and Reynolds are Privates Christian and Halton of the King's Own (Royal Lancaster Regiment). Three of row three are visible, left to right Corporal J. Hewitson VC, Private J. White VC and Lance-Sergeant T. F. Mayson VC all of the King's Own (Royal Lancaster Regiment). In the next row the tall officer is Second-Lieutenant J. Johnson VC, then Private E. Sykes VC and the small figure between White and Mayson is Private W. Wood VC, all of The Northumberland Fusiliers. The next row is Private A. Hutt and Captain R. E. Phillips both of The Royal Warwickshire Regiment. On the extreme left in the next row is Private S. F. Godley VC, Royal Fusiliers, who won the second VC of the Great War defending the Nimy railway bridge near Mons on 23 August 1914.

There were a total of nine groups. The smallest group was Group No. 1 with 24 VCs and the largest was Group No. 7 with 46 VCs. The Army, with most VCs, formed the most number of groups but the Royal Navy, as the senior service, headed the march in Group No. 1 together with the Royal Marines and the Royal Naval Reserve. The Royal Air Force, represented by three VC recipients, had become a separate service only two years before and was in Group No. 9 along with the Indian Army and Dominion Forces.

17. Modern day view outside the railings of Wellington Barracks looking down Birdcage Walk *(John Mulholland)*

The VCs assembled on the other side of these railings on the barrack square before setting out on the march. After leaving the barracks the procession turned right into Birdcage Walk. On the railings on the right is a memorial plaque to Gunner A. P. Sullivan VC who was accidentally killed at this spot on 9 April 1937 whilst serving as a representative of Australia during the coronation of HM King George VI.

Admiral of the Fleet Sir Arthur Wilson VC GCB OM GCVO led the naval VCs at the head of Group No. 1. In the front row with him were Lieutenant-Colonel L. Halliday VC CB (Royal Marine Light Infantry), Commander B. Guy VC DSO and Lieutenant-Commander N. Holbrook VC. In the second row were Captain E. Unwin VC CB CMG and Petty Officer G. Samson VC, both awarded VCs for gallantry at V Beach, Gallipoli (see photograph 14).

The Army VCs were grouped by regiment and this explains why the number of VCs in each group varied. The purpose was to keep comrades of the same regiment together (see photograph 16). Many regiments could boast a full turn out of their VC recipients, but others still had men serving abroad. For example, the only surviving VC recipient of the Manchester Regiment who did not attend was William Thomas Forshaw VC, who was then on active service in India.

The band of the Welsh Guards led the march and at the rear were 12 cars provided by the RAF to transport disabled VC recipients who were too elderly or unable to join the march. Approximately 20 VC recipients were in this category.

A complete listing of the VC recipients by group is shown in Appendix 1 where the marching order is shown. This was the planned marching list. Some of those listed were not present, some were present but chose not to march and the disabled VCs travelled by cars in the rear. Some VCs decided to omit the march altogether and these included General Sir Dighton Probyn VC and Lieutenant-General H.H. Lyster VC, both Mutiny veterans, who chose to go straight to the Palace.

The route of the march from Wellington Barracks was initially away from the Palace down Birdcage Walk. They turned left into Horse Guards Road, passed Horse Guards Parade and left into The Mall and down to the Palace (photographs 19 and 20). In effect, the march was around the edge of St James's Park. The route was one and a third miles long and allowing for average walking speed, the march took approximately 30 minutes.

Because of the paperwork delays at the Barracks and in assembling, the march did not commence until around 3.00 pm. The drums beat a preliminary roll and brass and cymbals of the Guards band crashed out the first few bars of a slow march and so the procession began. At that point there was a loud outburst of cheering from the large crowds who had gathered along the route. The enthusiastic cheering was sustained for much of the march.

18. Headlines of the Illustrated Sunday Herald, 27 June 1920 *(Illustrated Sunday Herald)*

A view of Group 1 during the march. See also photograph 14.

The Daily News reported:

> As they emerged into Birdcage-walk a roar of cheering went up, handkerchiefs flickered in the crowd, and hats were thrown in the air. Where the throng was particularly dense stood a lady holding a cardboard box filled with roses and carnations. As the procession passed she threw nosegays toward it. Alas: they fell short, but a police inspector on duty who remembered the story of Nelson and his blind eye, looked the other way while the lady gathered the fallen blossoms and passed them through the police cordon to the men.

The pace set by the band was a moderate one because of the age and infirmity of some of the VC holders. Ambulances were located at strategic positions along the route but they were not needed. Not a single VC holder had to fall out during the march.

Corporal Veale VC, who had travelled up from Devon, recorded:

> Thousands of people were cheering us; but I could not help noticing that some people were crying. We were happy and laughing, and I expect they were reminded of bereavements. One lady gave me a bouquet of flowers. "Good old Devon", she said, "I come from Crediton."

The VCs were genuinely surprised at the reception they received and the deafening cheering of the crowds. "It was a greeting I could not describe", said one VC afterwards, "and quite different from anything I have experienced since 1914. It made me feel proud of myself. I should have found it easier to cry than to laugh."

The Daily Mail gave a graphic description of the march:

> What a party it was! There were big men and little men, fat prosperous-looking men and frail youngsters, who might well have been rejected by the recruiting people as not reaching the required physical standard. Their deeds of valour covered all the fields and arts of war. To many the old word of command bridged the years between the return to civil occupation and the days of discipline.

> As the Column of Courage turned into Birdcage Walk an immense crowd, which had waited hours to see it, broke into a vociferous cheer, which followed the gallant company all the way to the Palace.

> The Navy in uniform came first. The crowd recognised its heroes individually, and those who did not know were helped to knowledge by representatives of the Services who were present in large bodies.

> There were shouts of "Holbrook!" No crowd bothers about rank. The man who dived under the Dardanelles looked uncomfortable. There were shouts, too, for "Carpenter" and "Good old Vindictive" - in fact, there was a continuous shouting of names and ships, which showed that the crowd was well versed in the Navy's heroism.

> Following the Navy came all the branches of the Army grouped in regiments. Some were in uniform, others in mufti. There were VCs in top-hats and spats and VCs in cloth caps and mufflers. Again names and regiments were shouted amid storms of approval. There were cries of "Good old O'Leary!" and the big Irishman, who laid out eight Germans with

a spade, smiled back appreciatively, while a big gathering of Jewish (*sic*) shouted for Issy Smith of the REs.

Drain and Luke, two neat figures in mufti, who saved the guns at Le Cateau in November (*sic*) 1914, marched side by side. There was Private Henry Robson, of the Royal Scots, the hero of Kemmel, who was being "chipped" by his mates on account of his white spats *(see photographs 16, 42 and 47).*

And so they marched, a modest body of men, who seemed to be divided between the necessity of march discipline and the desire to show the crowd which was honouring them in no uncertain manner that they appreciated the applause.

The crowd kept a special cheer for those who could not march. They came in a pathetic procession of motor cars. Some were sightless, some limbless. All were badly battered, but they all smiled bravely.

Sitting back in one of the cars was a hero with one eye covered with a bandage and one leg shot away, but he appeared to be revelling in the proceedings. He kept raising his hat, revealing a bald head and his jolly appearance moved the crowd to ecstasies. Finally, a young girl broke the police barrier, rushed up to the car, and, amid shrieks of applause, imprinted a kiss on the cheeks of the jolly hero.

Instinctively as the procession passed, the spectators bared their heads as a mark of respect. At times a touch of awe seemed to strike the crowds and give an air of solemnity to the scene, only to be broken by a louder outburst of cheering.

Sir Arthur Knyvet Wilson VC GCB OM GCVO

Admiral of the Fleet Sir Arthur Wilson VC was the most senior ranking VC recipient at the Garden Party. He led the march to the Palace at the head of Group No. 1.

During the advance at the Battle of El Teb, in Sudan, on 29 February 1884 Captain Wilson of HMS *Hecla* attached himself to the Naval Brigade in place of a Lieutenant who was mortally wounded. As the troops closed on the enemy, the Arabs charged the battery detachment which was dragging one of its guns. Captain Wilson then engaged in single combat with some of the enemy and so protected the detachment until men of the York and Lancaster Regiment came to his assistance. For his courageous action he was awarded the VC.

Wilson became Admiral in Command Channel Fleet in 1905 and was promoted to Admiral of the Fleet in 1907. He was First Sea Lord and Senior Naval Lord of the Admiralty 1910-1912. Although he retired in 1912, he was recalled to the Admiralty during the First World War. Sir Arthur Wilson died, aged 79, in May 1921, eleven months after the Garden Party.

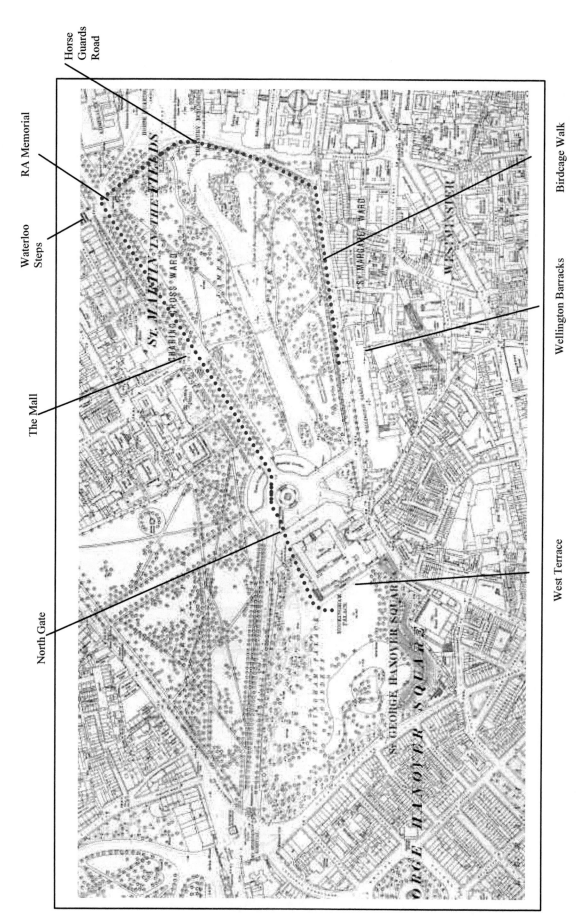

19. Map of the route of the march from Wellington Barracks to Buckingham Palace
(Reproduced from the 1916 Ordnance Survey map)

The VC march left Wellington Barracks turned right and went eastwards down Birdcage Walk away from the Palace; left again at the RA Memorial down The Mall entering the Palace grounds by the North Gate. This map was published in 1916 and can be compared with an aerial view taken in 2000 on the next page.

Horse Guards Road

RA Memorial

Waterloo Steps

The Mall

North Gate

Birdcage Walk

Wellington Barracks

West Terrace

26

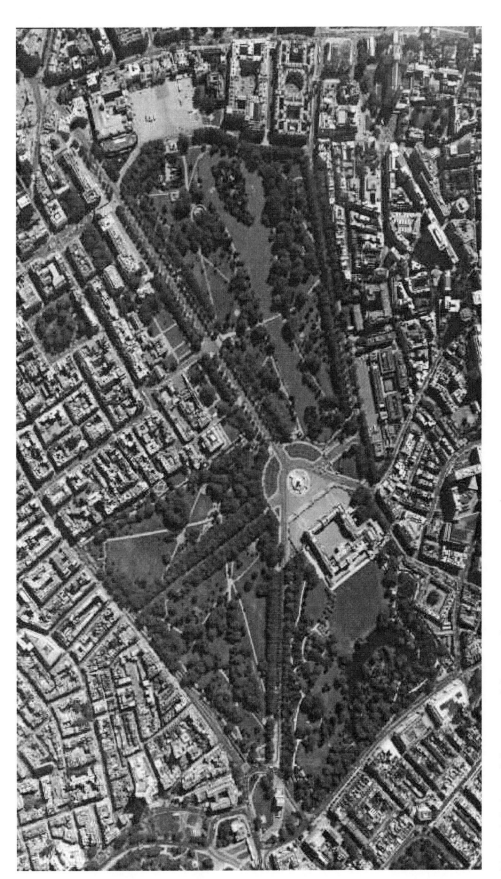

20. Aerial view of the route of the march (*Aerofilms*)

This is an aerial view taken in 2000 showing Wellington Barracks, the route of the march and the Gardens of Buckingham Palace.

27

One Royal Artillery VC recipient wrote later in *The Gunner* :

> We are an inarticulate people - apt to be shy, and look uncomfortable when heroics are in the air; and, to the astonishment of our neighbours, to appear not a little relieved when a joke, or the latest music hall refrain, puts us back in more familiar atmosphere; but deep down the spirit is there; else had we faltered, and failed in the fight; and to it folk gave expression that Saturday afternoon, not so much in the cheers that rang out, though they were good to hear, as in the spontaneous baring of heads when the King's guests went down to the Palace.

As the VC recipients had marched down Birdcage Walk a member of the public joined the column, almost unseen. Sir Percival Marling VC was marching in Group 7, near the end of the procession and recalled the incident in his autobiography[5]:

> As we were going down Birdcage Walk a man from the crowd joined the section in front of me, unseen by the police, and talked to a Tommy, apparently a pal of his. I said to the man next to me, "Do you see that fellow who has just chipped in? I don't believe he has any right to be here." The man, however, walked along till we got to Buckingham Palace gates, and then went in with the procession. Directly we got inside the gates I called a policeman and told him our suspicions. The bobby went up to the man and found, as we thought, that he hadn't got a VC, and he was promptly turned out.

As the VCs marched past the Waterloo Steps[6] the crowd there noticed that the staff of the German Embassy had come out to see the procession pass and that one member had not removed his hat. Though the crowd booed and called to him to take it off he remained with his hat on (see photograph 22).

Colonel Sir Percival Marling Bt. VC CB.

Sir Percival Marling VC was commissioned into the KRRC in August 1880 and served throughout the Boer War of 1880-81. Between 1882 and 1884 he was on continuous operations in Egypt and Sudan and was awarded the VC for saving the life of a wounded private of The Royal Sussex Regiment in Sudan in March 1884.

Marling served for much of the war in South Africa between 1899 and 1902 and received a CB for his services. In 1902 he was promoted to command 18th Hussars. Marling was forced to retire in 1910 when he was injured by a horse while on duty. However, at the outbreak of the First World War he volunteered for active service and in September 1914 crossed to France where he served on the HQ staff of the Indian Army Corps. Marling's autobiography, *Rifleman and Hussar*, was published in 1931 and he died in May 1936. His VC group was auctioned by Spink of London on 8 November 1994 for £29,700.

---

[5] *Rifleman and Hussar*, John Murray, London, 1931.

[6] The Waterloo Steps lead from The Mall up to Waterloo Place which leads into Pall Mall. The German Embassy was located nearby.

21. Group Nos 2 and 3 marching to Buckingham Palace *(Daily Sketch)*

The three officers on the right are the last row of Group 2, left to right Lieutenant-Colonel. H. N. Schofield VC, Lieutenant. A.O. Pollard VC MC DCM and Lieutenant R.L. Haine VC MC. Next is the first row of Group 3. The civilian with a hat is Sapper A. Archibald VC. Behind him is General Sir Reginald Hart VC KCB KCVO, wearing two Royal Humane Society Medals on his right breast. Three rows behind Hart, wearing a straw bowler, is Sergeant O. Brooks VC.

22. Modern day view of the Waterloo Steps *(John Mulholland)*

This view is taken from the Royal Artillery Memorial (see photograph 23).

Opposite the Waterloo Steps at the junction of The Mall and Horse Guards Road is the Royal Artillery Memorial (see photographs 19 and 23). The memorial commemorates the 1,000 men of the Royal Artillery who died in South Africa in 1899-1902. Sir Aston Webb, architect of the nearby Admiralty Arch, was appointed as architect and the memorial was unveiled in 1910. The memorial would have been a place of pride to the 18 VCs of the Royal Artillery marching past and six of these were awarded their VCs for South Africa: Alfred Ind, Isaac Lodge, George Nurse, Edmund Phipps-Hornby, Hamilton Reed and Harry Schofield, who can be seen in the foreground of photograph 21.

The *Sunday Express* reported:

> It was a colourless pageant, something drab and commonplace to the eye, but the quick imagination of the spectators invested the little procession with a beauty and glory more radiant than the dyer or the weaver of fine gold could lend.

The crowd, though not dense everywhere, was thick on The Mall with more men than women. The *Sunday Express* estimated there were five men to every two women. The crowds were thickest near the Palace gates where the cheering was deafening (see photographs 24, 25 and 26).

23. Modern day view of the Royal Artillery Memorial, The Mall
(John Mulholland)

Located at the junction of Horse Guards Road and The Mall opposite the Waterloo steps.

24. Marching down The Mall and turning right at the Victoria Memorial
(The Weekly Dispatch)

The VCs after leaving The Mall turning right at the Victoria Memorial before entering the North Gate of Buckingham Palace. Group No. 1 (Naval VCs) lead the march.

An *Evening Standard* correspondent at the Queen Victoria Memorial reported:

> The scene from the Victoria Memorial, looking down the Mall, was wonderfully impressive. Masses of people on either side of the route and in front of the Palace had waited patiently for over two hours to see this procession.
>
> Right down to the Admiralty Arch and past the Palace at the other end they stood. Suddenly the sound of the band became clearer. When the heads of the marchers appeared handkerchiefs flickered along the crowd. The cheering became a great roar. Men waved their hats and women blew kisses. On they came. They marched so proudly and so splendidly that the crowd fairly rose at them.

The King and Queen, Princess Mary and the Duke of Connaught stepped out onto the balcony opposite the North Gate. From there they had an excellent view of the procession advancing down The Mall. As he watched, the King noticed how dense the crowd was around the Palace and that the tiers of steps around the Queen Victoria Memorial were being kept clear of spectators by the police. He immediately sent out an urgent order to the superintendents that the public were to enjoy the advantage of these raised positions. These steps were immediately filled by appreciative crowds (see photograph 25).

A number of wounded soldiers, still wearing their hospital blue, had places specially reserved near the garden entrance as did some little girls, wearing bright scarlet cloaks, from the Guards' Girls School.

31

25. Marching past the Victoria Memorial *(The Illustrated London News Picture Library)*

The procession of VC recipients approaching the North Gate of Buckingham Palace passing the Queen Victoria Memorial. Just about to enter the Gate is the band of the Welsh Guards. Behind them is the small naval contingent with their white caps visible. The King and Queen can just be seen on the balcony with the Queen's light coloured dress standing out. The ground is wet with puddles. The mass of spectators is thickest at this point in the march with some stood on the rim of the fountain wall. This photograph is in fact two images joined together - the vertical join line can be seen in the centre of the photograph.

26. Group No. 9 about to enter the Palace gates
(Photograph courtesy of the Imperial War Museum, London. Q66187)

This photograph, taken from the Victoria Memorial, shows the rear part of Group No. 9.

32

The Times correspondent suggested that the ordeal of the march was too much for some VCs:

> ... the little band of heroes passed between densely-crowded masses of people, who cheered them lustily, until they passed inside the gates of Buckingham Palace. Here, in a quieter atmosphere, many of them heaved a sigh of relief. They are shy men, these heroes, and to many of them this march through the streets was an ordeal with which they would willingly have dispensed: indeed the number of absentees made one wonder if the courage of some of them had not failed them at the last moment. Many were there who carried the bronze cross in their pockets until the moment arrived when it had to be produced, and it went back to the pocket again at the earliest opportunity. While there may have been some who were expected, but who did not take part in the march, quite a number who for one reason or another were regarded as unlikely to be present were in their places when the line was re-formed in the Buckingham Palace grounds.

After cheering the heroes into the grounds of the Palace at around 3.30 pm the crowd turned their attention to the Royal party on the balcony. Cheer after cheer was raised, which the King and Queen acknowledged by bowing. They then left the balcony to make their way down to the gardens to join their guests.

27. Entering the Palace grounds *(Illustrated Sunday Herald)*

The VCs marching through the North Gate of Buckingham Palace. The royal party can be seen on the balcony overlooking the North Gate.

6 Buckingham Palace and Gardens

The gardens of Buckingham Palace have been described as a walled oasis in the middle of London. They cover 39 acres and are bounded by Constitution Hill, Grosvenor Place, Lower Grosvenor Place and Buckingham Gate (photographs 19 and 20). The gardens are informal in design and include a large lawn sweeping down from the West Terrace to a lake which includes an island. The garden is home to a great variety of wildlife including 30 types of bird and over 350 different types of wild flower.

The design of the gardens dates back to 1825, when George IV transformed Buckingham Palace into a royal residence and appointed William Townsend Aiton, head of the Royal Botanic Gardens at Kew, to oversee the modelling of the grounds into a naturalistic landscape. King William IV had ambivalent feelings about the Palace. First he suggested that it might make admirable barracks for the Foot Guards but the offer was refused by Lord Grey on account of the expense. Later King William reluctantly sanctioned the building of Wellington Barracks for the Guards and their iron railings still bear his royal cypher, "W R IV", with the date 1833. King William[7] then tried to offer the Palace as a gift to Parliament when the Houses of Parliament burned down in 1834. But this offer was declined by the Prime Minister, Lord Melbourne.

28. Modern day aerial view of Buckingham Palace and part of the gardens
(Reproduced by kind permission of Jarrold Publishing)

The VCs marched through the North Gate on the right, passed the King and Queen on the balcony and entered the gardens via the North Lodge middle right of the photograph near parked cars. The extensive lawn can be seen at the top with part of the lake visible.

---

[7] One of King William IV's great grandsons, Charles Fitzclarence, was awarded his VC for gallantry at Mafeking in October 1899. Fitzclarence, who was killed in action on 10 November 1914, was the grandson of George, 1st Earl of Munster, who was the eldest of five illegitimate sons sired by King William and borne by the actress Mrs Jordan.

29. Modern day view of Buckingham Palace and gardens *(Falcon Crest)*

This aerial view shows the West Terrace and lawn with the gardens and lake. Wellington Barracks are shown upper right. The white building is the Guards chapel built in 1960s to replace the original chapel destroyed by a flying bomb on 18 June 1944. To the right of the chapel is the Home Office. The entire route march is visible on this photograph and Horse Guards can be seen top left centre. On the right hand perimeter of the lawn some marquées are visible for a garden function.

When Victoria became Queen in 1837 she decided that the Palace would suit her well and it became an official royal residence. Early in her reign the tradition of afternoon Garden Parties was established. They were known as 'breakfasts' and were popular in high society in the mid nineteenth century as described in several of Trollope's novels. With the death of Prince Albert, the Royal Consort, all the royal parties were abruptly ended and did not resume for over six years. Towards the end of Queen Victoria's reign much of the organising of entertainment fell to her son, the Prince of Wales (later King Edward VII).

Garden parties were reintroduced on a much larger scale by King George V and Queen Mary. E. S. Turner wrote[8]:

> In further recognition of social changes, the King developed the garden parties which his grandmother had initiated. These were designed to admit thousands, when 'Courts' could receive only hundreds. An invitation to a garden party did not count as a presentation at Court, but it was a widely sought honour.

---

[8] *The Court of St. James*, E. S. Turner, Michael Joseph, 1959.

30. A 1930s view of Buckingham Palace's West Terrace and lawn from the lake
(Topical Press)

Since the Second World War the soot-blackened stone has been cleaned as seen
in photograph 31.

**31. Modern day view of Buckingham Palace's West Terrace and lawn from the
lake** *(Andrew Lawson)*

Compare this photograph with photograph 30. A semi-circular dome has been
added above the Bow Room and Music Room.

37

32. The Grand Entrance of Buckingham Palace from the Principal Entrance *(Topical Press)*

On their way to the West Terrace the guests passed through the Principal Entrance, across the courtyard and into the Grand Entrance. For an aerial view see photograph 28.

Few citizens had suspected that Buckingham Palace could boast an attractive rear elevation, and such extensive and attractive gardens. The procedure was for the Royal Family to circulate without excessive formality among the guests, and then retire into a Durbar tent (the famous Shamiana) for special presentations. A rained-out Garden Party provided cruel amusement for the Press, for it was impossible to admit thousands of dripping guests into the Palace.

The 1920 VC Garden Party entertained approximately one thousand people including VC recipients, their guests, the Royal Family, distinguished politicians, leaders of the armed services, courtiers and representatives of the Press.

This would have been a relatively modest gathering compared to the royal garden parties of today. Typically, HM The Queen hosts three parties each year and 10,000 guests are invited to each. In recent years parts of the gardens have become accessible when Buckingham Palace opens to the public for four weeks each summer.

33. The Grand Hall of Buckingham Palace *(Topical Press)*

The guests entered the Grand Hall from the left and walked up the steps on the right, through the Marble Hall into the Bow Room and out onto the West Terrace.

In June 2002 HM The Queen hosted two concerts on the lawn to commemorate her Golden Jubilee. Each concert was attended by 12,000 visitors and seen on television by a world-wide audience of 200 million. So the gardens still play an important role, as they did in 1920, in making it possible for the Sovereign to entertain a large number of guests.

In the 1920 Garden Party most of the activity took place on the West Terrace and the lawn. From the French windows it is possible to step onto the West Terrace which runs for 150 yards under Nash's west façade of the Palace. From this position most of the garden can be seen. The balustrade of the West Terrace is made of Coade Stone as are the elaborate urns. Ten wide steps lead from the terrace down to the gravel path and onto the lawn. At the foot of these steps the VC recipients were individually presented to the King and Queen. Senior military figures and members of the Royal Family stood at a discreet distance on the steps and many courtiers and distinguished visitors stood on the Terrace itself (see photograph 42).

Shortly after the march started the relatives and guests walked from the Barracks to Buckingham Palace. They entered by the Main Gate and walked through the arches of the Principal Entrance, across the Quadrangle and into the Palace itself by the Grand Entrance (see photographs 28 and 32). They then passed through the Grand Hall and up the staircase across the Marble Hall and into the Bow Room (see photograph 33). From the Bow Room the relatives and guests then walked directly into the West Terrace and down the steps onto the lawn where court officials assembled them in lines facing the West Terrace to await the arrival of the VCs.

On arrival at the gardens, the VC recipients paraded on the lawn between the guests and the West Terrace. The marquées were positioned at the edge of the lake and at the eastern perimeter of the lawn. Although the guests of the VCs passed through the Palace on their way to the gardens, during the party the Palace was not accessible and at the end of the day everyone departed by the North Gate at the front of the Palace.

7 Inspection by the King

In contrast to the cheering crowds outside the gates not a sound was heard from relatives gathered on the lawn. The *Daily Express* reported:

> There are moments when it is impossible to voice the feelings that surge within, and this was one of them. Many of those present must have thought of the mothers and fathers who stood beside them and wore the Maltese Cross on their right breast, signifying that their loved ones had given their lives in gaining undying fame.
>
> A brigadier-general gave the command "Halt!" and the VCs stood perfectly still until they were asked to fall in under their respective sections in order of seniority of award *(to be inspected by the King)*.

The VCs stood in front of their relatives facing the steps of the West Terrace. The new groupings were in accordance with official lists prepared for the occasion and seniority was based on the date of *The London Gazette* notification and not the date of the VC deed, which could have been several years earlier as in the case of CSM Evans who was last in line. Each VC recipient had been given a card which was to be handed to the court official on duty. The card gave the name of the VC so that he could be correctly announced and also stated the group to which the recipient was to proceed.

There were seven groups, A to G, with the letters of each group shown on high poles to make re-marshalling easier. Even so, it could not have been an easy task. Court officials arranged the VCs two deep in their respective groups to be inspected by the King.

The groups were:

A   The Indian Mutiny, 1857 to April 1899
B   1900 - 1905
C   1914 - 1915
D   1916
E   1917
F   January - November 1918
G   December 1918 to January 1920

While court officials helped the VCs to their correct places, the RAF cars carrying the 20 disabled VCs arrived on the gravelled path in front of the West Terrace. Men of the Royal Army Medical Corps and the Corps of Commissionaires stepped forward with wheelchairs for those requiring assistance. Only a few took up the offer.

34. King George V begins the inspection of the VCs on the lawn of Buckingham Palace *(The Royal Collection, © 2007 Her Majesty Queen Elizabeth II)*

The royal party has six figures: behind the King is his uncle, the Duke of Connaught, partially hidden and wearing a black arm band for his recently deceased daughter, Margaret. In the second row on the left is Prince Albert (later King George VI) partially hidden by the Duke of Connaught. Second row right is Prince Henry, the third son of the King, later to be the Duke of Gloucester. Back row left is Prince Arthur of Connaught and the Marquis of Carisbrooke.

The order of inspection is Lieutenant-General H. H. Lyster VC CB, the oldest VC present, in his plumed hat, Private J. Williams VC and Colonel J. W. Chaplin VC CB. The fourth in line should have been General Sir Reginald Hart VC KCB KCVO but it appears to be Private S. Wassall VC followed by Hart who can be seen wearing the Royal Humane Society Medals on his right breast. Eighth in line is Admiral of the Fleet Sir Arthur Wilson VC with his peaked white naval cap and sword hanging forward. The relatives are stood in line behind the VCs. See photograph 35.

Once assembled, the VCs waited in silence for the arrival of the King. In this interval, the Secretary of State for War, Mr Winston Churchill MP[9], walked across the lawn - a solitary figure attracting the attention of the crowd. *The Observer* reported he "looked aloof and Napoleonic". Churchill would have found the tranquillity of the garden in contrast to the hectic demands of Government. The War Office had to deal with many problems at the time: the deepening crisis in

---

[9] Churchill was also Secretary of State for Air and held both appointments since January 1919. Although responsible for two separate ministries he had been informed by the Prime Minister, David Lloyd George, that he would receive only one salary.

Ireland, an insurrection in Iraq and the threat of the Bolshevik revolution spreading across the border into Poland.

Among invited guests, with Churchill on the upper terrace, were members of the Royal Household including the Duke of York, Prince Henry, Princess Mary, the Duke of Connaught, Prince and Princess Arthur of Connaught, Princess Beatrice, Princess Christian, the Duchess of Albany, the Marquess and Marchioness of Carisbrooke, Princess Marie Louise and the Dowager Countess of Airlie.

35. King George V begins the inspection of the VCs with their relatives behind them
(Illustrated Sunday Herald)

A wider angle view of photograph 34 showing the relatives of the VCs lined up behind and a member of the Corps of Commissionaires standing by with the bathchairs for Lieutenant-General Lyster VC CB and other frail VC recipients.

Also present were Admiral Sir Doveton Sturdee, Admiral Colville, Field Marshal Earl Haig[10], Field Marshal Sir William Robertson, Lord Methuen, Air Marshal Sir Hugh Trenchard, the Hon. Charlotte Knollys, Viscountess Sandhurst and others (see photograph 37). The King's Indian orderly officers were also present.

Almost immediately after the VCs were drawn up in double line, the King and Queen stepped out of the Palace onto the West Terrace and took their places at the top of the flight of steps. With the King and Queen were the Duke of York, in the uniform of the Royal Air Force, Prince Henry and Princess Mary. The National Anthem was played and the King, wearing the service dress uniform of a Field Marshal, complete with ceremonial sword and riding boots, walked down the carpeted steps onto the lawn and inspected each line in turn. He was accompanied by the Duke of Connaught, Prince Albert the Duke of York, Prince Henry, Prince Arthur of Connaught and the Marquis of Carisbrooke (see photograph 34).

---

[10] Field Marshal Sir Douglas Haig was created first Earl Haig in 1919. He received the thanks of Parliament and £100,000 (equivalent to £2.5 million today).

The actual order of the line of VC recipients did not correspond with the official list as photograph 34 shows. The first in line should have been General Sir Dighton Probyn VC GCB GCSI GCVO ISO. Although present in the gardens he chose not to be included - possibly because he was infirm and at 87 found it difficult to stand for long. However, this did not deter another Indian Mutiny VC present, Lieutenant-General H. H. Lyster VC CB, who moved from his bathchair to be included as first in the inspection (see photograph 34). Next in the line-up should have been Colonel J. W. Chaplin VC CB followed by Pte. J. Williams VC of Rorke's Drift fame and then General Sir Reginald Hart VC KCB KCVO. However, photograph 34 shows that after Lyster was Williams, then Chaplin, then an unidentified recipient followed by Hart. The unidentified recipient is likely to be Private S. Wassall VC, one of the few survivors of the disaster at Isandhlwana in 1879.

Lt. General Harry Hammon Lyster VC CB

Lieutenant Lyster, serving with the 72nd Bengal Native Infantry, won his VC during the Indian Mutiny. On 23 May 1858, at Calpee, he charged alone and broke the skirmishing square of the retreating rebel army and killed two or three sepoys in the engagement. Lyster served throughout the Mutiny and also saw action in Afghanistan.

He was promoted to Lieutenant-General in 1891 but was placed on the unemployed supernumerary list the following year. He later became an officer of the King's Corps of Gentlemen-at-Arms* and wore the Corps' distinctive scarlet gold-braided uniform with plumed hat to the Garden Party (see photograph 34). He was the oldest VC present and the second man to be presented to the King and Queen. Lt. General Lyster died in February 1922, aged 91.

* Non-combatant troops, chosen from decorated officers in the armed forces. They act in attendance of the Sovereign at coronations, state openings of parliament, receptions, royal garden parties and state visits.

Further on, the line is out of order by a fair margin. Admiral of the Fleet Sir Arthur Wilson should have been seventeenth in line but is in eighth position (see photograph 34 where his sword, beard and white naval cap can be seen).

The lines of VC recipients proudly waiting to be inspected presented a unique spectacle in the history of the VC which spanned 61 years between awards from Lyster gazetted in 1859 to Evans in 1920. Some of the VCs were in uniform while others were in civilian clothing, wearing a variety of headwear from top-hats to bowlers and straw boaters. Generals and admirals stood to attention next to privates and ordinary seamen. It was a colourful display reflecting the history of Britain and her Empire; scarlet tunics with gold braid, khaki uniforms of more recent wars, a variety of civilian dress contrasting with naval blue dress uniforms.

A royal photographer and members of the press were at hand to record the event. The inspection took only a few minutes with the King pausing occasionally to ask a question.

The Queen, who was wearing a dress of Wedgewood blue crêpe de chine, with a brocaded design, and a blue and silver toque, remained on the steps with the other ladies while the King conducted the inspection. With the Queen were Princess Christian and her two daughters, Princess Victoria and Princess Marie Louise; Princess Louise Duchess of Argyll, Princess Beatrice, the Duchess of Albany, Princess Arthur of Connaught and Lady Carisbrooke.

As the King returned from the inspection, the Queen joined him at the foot of the steps for the individual presentations. At that point an agitated ciné-operator was trying to find a suitable place to record the event. The King noticed the man's anxiety and, much to the cameraman's amazement and pleasure, the King called him over to point out a good vantage point.

Immediately before the presentations began, it suddenly began to rain heavily threatening to spoil the whole event. The King laughed but made no effort to seek shelter, reassuring those who were inclined to rush to the marquées. Officials quickly produced umbrellas for the Queen and Princess Mary and many ran for shelter. The King and Queen smiled and kept their places until the three minute shower ceased. Then the presentations began.

The Royal Princes

The Prince of Wales, later King Edward VIII, was not present at the Garden Party as he was on an official tour of Australia and New Zealand. While in Australia he visited Government House and met 11 Australian VCs.

Prince Albert, the Duke of York, had received this title in the King's Birthday Honours three weeks before the Garden Party. He was the second son of King George V and was later to become King George VI following the abdication of his brother in 1936. He took part in the inspection of the VCs accompanying his father (see photograph 34). The Duke of York can be seen more clearly in photograph 37 standing on the West Terrace steps during the presentations.

Prince Henry, the third son of King George V was a career soldier. He also took part in the inspection of the VCs with his father. Prince Henry can be seen clearly on the right of photograph 34 and next to Prince Albert on the steps in photograph 37. He later became the Duke of Gloucester and married Lady Alice, daughter of the Duke of Buccleuch in 1935. The Duke died in 1974. His widow, Princess Alice, HRH The Duchess of Gloucester, born in 1901, became the longest lived member of the Royal Family. She was presented to Court in 1920 but did not attend the Garden Party and died in October 2004, aged 102.

8 Presentation to the King and Queen

The formality of the presentation was undertaken by General Sir Douglas Dawson and Major Seymour, who in a clear resonant voice, announced each VC recipient's name, rank, regiment, campaign or theatre of war for which the decoration was awarded and the date of notification. Standing immediately to the right of the King, Sir Douglas kept his arm extended in front of the file, allowing only one to pass at a time. He cocked his head and listened smilingly to the conversation that followed. When the VC had passed on the next in line was allowed forward (see photograph 42).

The King and Queen shook hands with each man as he passed and said a few words to most of them. The procession was led by General Sir Dighton Probyn, who was awarded the VC in June 1858 for bravery at the Battle of Agra. He was brought in his bathchair but insisted on marching the last 20 yards. Putting an affectionate arm around his shoulder, the King remonstrated with his grand old servant (see photographs 36 and 44). They spoke with him for some time. Following Probyn, in the scarlet gold-braided uniform and plumed hat of an officer of the King's Corps of Gentlemen-at-Arms, was Lieutenant-General H. H. Lyster, another Indian Mutiny veteran, who single-handedly charged and broke a skirmishing square of rebels. After being presented, these two elderly veterans returned to their chairs where they watched their fellow VCs come past, the majority of whom were immediately seized upon by admiring relatives who wanted to know what the King and Queen had said to them.

36. Sir Dighton Probyn VC is presented to King George V
(The Royal Collection, © 2007 Her Majesty Queen Elizabeth II)

Sir Dighton Probyn VC was very frail but left his bath chair and marched 20 yards to be presented to the King and Queen. Behind Probyn's head can be seen the plumed hat of Lieutenant-General H. H. Lyster VC who was second-in-line and awaiting his presentation to the King.

Sir Dighton Probyn VC GCB GCSI GCVO ISO

Of all the guests present none had served the Royal Family as faithfully, or as long, as General Sir Dighton Probyn VC. In 1872 he was appointed Equerry, and five years later Comptroller and Treasurer of the Household of King Edward, then Prince of Wales. On the accession of King Edward VII to the throne in 1901 he continued his duties with the title of Keeper of the Privy Purse. He also held the appointment of Extra Equerry and was a member of the Councils of the Duchies of Lancaster and Cornwall, and secretary to the Royal Victorian Order. After the death of King Edward in 1910 Sir Dighton became Extra Equerry to King George V and also Comptroller of the Household of Queen Alexandra.

Although Sir Dighton Probyn was the longest serving VC recipient at the time of the Garden Party, he was not the oldest. That distinction was held by Lieutenant-General Lyster, who at 89 was two years older than Probyn.

Probyn served the Royal Family loyally for over 50 years and was a much loved character. 'Dear Old Probyn', as he was affectionately known, died at Sandringham in June 1924, aged 91. He wore his VC with pride, but it was said that few had ever seen the decoration as it was well hidden under his long white beard. However, some of his orders, decorations and medals are visible in photograph 44. These were sold at auction by Dix Noonan Webb for £160,000 on 23 September 2005.

After Colonel John Chaplin (China 1860) came John Williams who won his VC for the gallant defence of the hospital at Rorke's Drift in January 1879. General Sir O'Moore Creagh VC GCB GCSI, co-editor of the celebrated reference work *The VC and DSO*, was presented to the King immediately after Private Wassall, one of the few survivors of Isandhlwana. Also present was General Sir Reginald Hart, who had won his VC in Afghanistan, in January 1879. The King and Queen shook hands with each man in turn, moving through the history of the Victoria Cross from the Indian Mutiny through the Boer War and the Great War to Russia in 1919. A full list of the theoretical order of the presentation is shown in Appendix 2.

Admiral of the Fleet Sir Arthur Wilson VC GCB OM GCVO, the senior officer present, who had won his VC at the Battle of El Teb in 1884, was theoretically the seventeenth man to be presented to the King. Immediately behind Sir Arthur Wilson was Sir Percival Marling VC who recorded his presentation in his autobiography:

> We passed singly before Their Majesties, and the King and Queen shook hands with each of us, and said a few gracious words. The Queen said to me, "How is it you are not marching with my regiment?" I replied, "I am very sorry, ma'am, here is the order of the proceedings, and I have to walk with His Majesty's Regiment, The King's Royal Rifle Corps, in which I got the VC". Admiral Wilson went past exactly in front of me. I hadn't seen him since Suakin, when he got his VC at the battle of El Teb in 1884. We had a great talk together.

In 1902 Marling had been given command of the 18th Hussars, later re-named 18th (Queen Mary's Own) Hussars which explains Queen Mary's question. As Marling pointed out to the Queen, the VCs were told to march with the unit in which they were awarded the VC.

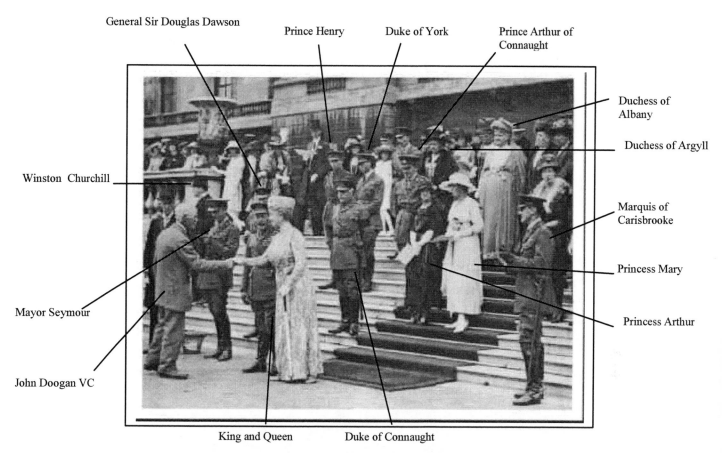

General Sir Douglas Dawson

Prince Henry

Duke of York

Prince Arthur of Connaught

Duchess of Albany

Duchess of Argyll

Winston Churchill

Marquis of Carisbrooke

Princess Mary

Mayor Seymour

Princess Arthur

John Doogan VC

King and Queen

Duke of Connaught

37. Private John Doogan VC, thirteenth in line, is presented to Queen Mary
(The Royal Collection © 2007 Her Majesty Queen Elizabeth II)

For a commentary of this scene and a wider angle view see photograph 38.

38. Private John Doogan VC shakes hands with Queen Mary
(The Illustrated London News Picture Library)

This is a wider angle view of photograph 37. Notice the number of guests on the West Terrace. Prince Albert, the Duke of York, the future King George VI, is standing on the fifth step, behind the King and Queen. Princess Mary, in the white dress, is on the third step of the red carpet. In the line of VCs waiting to be presented, the distinctive figure of Admiral of the Fleet Sir Arthur Wilson VC can be clearly seen. Immediately behind him is Sir Percival Marling VC. If the VCs were presented in the correct order the white-haired VC shaking hands with the Queen should be Private John Doogan VC (see pages 67 and 68) and the VC waiting to be presented, in the striped tie, appears to be Private J. Murray. Pte J. Osborne VC (see photograph 12) was gazetted the same day as Doogan and Murray but it appears he had been presented before Doogan.

39. Piper Findlater VC is presented to Queen Mary *(The Sphere)*

Left to right: Court Official, Findlater, Major Seymour, General Sir Douglas Dawson, Queen Mary, Duke of Connaught and higher on the steps, the Duke of York (later King George VI). King George V is virtually hidden by Queen Mary in this photograph.

As the long file passed the King had a personal message for each VC. An old private in mufti had his VC hidden away on his waistcoat. The King, as he talked with him, smilingly chided his modesty and opened his coat to show him how he should flaunt the honour his courage had won. The *Evening Standard* reporter recorded:

> This was no perfunctory ceremony, cold with formalism. These were men the King was delighted to honour, and his delight and pride were made clear.

50

Piper George Findlater VC of The Gordon Highlanders was warmly welcomed by the King and Queen (see photograph 39). As he approached the King a reel was played by the pipe band.

Piper George Findlater VC

George Findlater enlisted in The Gordon Highlanders in 1888 and in 1896 was promoted to Piper in the Regimental band. His duty was to play stirring tunes on the bagpipes while leading his battalion into action.

On 20 October 1897 during the attack on the Dargai Heights, on the North West Frontier, Piper Findlater was shot through both feet and was unable to stand. He propped himself against a boulder and continued playing the Regimental March to encourage the advance. His courage under fire earned him the VC.

He was discharged due to his wounds on 17 May 1898, three days after receiving his award from Queen Victoria. On his return home he found his exploits had made him a national hero, and he was approached by music halls to play his pipes on stage. These musical acts were frowned upon by the military authorities, who halted further appearances. Public opinion was behind Findlater, however, and as a result the pension paid to VC recipients was increased from £10 to £50 per year.

Findlater re-enlisted in The Gordon Highlanders in 1914 but was discharged after being wounded at Loos in 1915. He died in 1942, aged 70.

The Manchester Guardian recorded:

> The South African list was a long one, and the men took a long time to pass, so leisurely was the King in his conversation with them. He asked one VC, who had saved a gun in face of desperate odds, what he was doing now, and when the man replied he was a miner, the King said, "That's right, we want more coal".

Captain J. G. Smyth VC (later Brigadier Sir John Smyth VC) who had won his VC in May 1915 during the Battle of Festubert, remembered[11] Queen Mary with great fondness:

> Their Majesties received every VC separately. I think my most abiding memory of the occasion was the grace and beauty of Her Majesty Queen Mary. She was so obviously thrilled and delighted and communicated her pleasure to everyone around her.

Several of the presentations were very poignant; like those of Captain E. B. B. Towse VC and Captain A. Buchanan VC MC. They had both been blinded in the service of their country - Towse in the Boer War and Buchanan in the Great War. Both were warmly welcomed by the King and Queen.

---

[11] *Milestones,* Sidgwick and Jackson, 1979.

Many of the VCs were in uniform and in every instance where they were in civilian dress the King enquired if they were suitably employed. *The Daily Herald*, not known for its support of royalty, had a reporter present and even he conceded:

> I want to insist on the fact that, while the King passed on the "brass hats" with a handshake and a nod, he kept most of the rank and file in conversation for a minute or two. Whether or not he persuaded them to tell him how hard life is for the demobilised here, I do not know - but I think he wanted that information.

The King had every reason to be concerned about whether his subjects were suitably employed. The post-war depression had brought about a rise in unemployment and in 1920 the number of out-of-work had reached 1,250,000. Many demobilised servicemen found it difficult to obtain work - including VC recipients. At the time of the Garden Party a number of VC guests were having real difficulty in finding regular employment including Samuel Harvey, Daniel Laidlaw, Robert Ryder and Issy Smith.

Another contemporary newspaper reported that "Employers generally are fighting shy of VC men, thinking that their psychology unfits them for civil employment". This view was confirmed by the experiences of several out-of-work VC recipients. For example, Alfred Pollard VC later wrote an article in the *Dundee Evening Telegraph* under the heading "VCs Don't Help to get Jobs". In it he wrote that "War heroes are distrusted now: even the pawnbrokers set a low value on decorations."

The Daily Herald reporter continued:

> Certainly there were plenty of hardships represented in the gathering. Some of the men were pitiful in their obvious attempts to make a brave show in honour of the occasion. So many tired suits of clothes had been so obviously renovated for that one day. And though they may have shaken hands with the King and eaten his strawberries and cream on Saturday, I fancy they will be wondering what chance they stand of getting a job this morning.

Many names announced by the King's Chamberlain caused a stir on the terrace steps and amongst the visitors. Everyone was anxious to get a glimpse of heroes who were household names. Through it all the bands, including that of the Welsh Guards, played a medley of popular themes and marches.

In the original Warrant for the VC it was possible to forfeit the VC for convicted criminal behaviour. Of the eight forfeited VCs, seven died prior to June 1920. The eighth VC, George Ravenhill, died in April 1921 and his name did not appear on the invitation lists nor was he present. However, a man who was recommended for forfeiture, but did not lose his VC, did attend. Edmund Fowler, then a private in the 2nd Battalion, The Cameronians (Scottish Rifles) won his VC on Zlobane Mountain in Zululand in March 1879. In 1887 he was found guilty of embezzling money from a fellow soldier and under the terms of the VC Warrant should have forfeited his decoration. But Queen Victoria, in her Golden Jubilee year, could not bring herself to sign the forfeiture submission. Fowler had already been reduced to the ranks and the Queen felt that if he was considered fit to serve in her Army he was fit to retain his VC. Colour Sergeant Fowler VC attended the 1920 Garden Party and because of his seniority of award was the sixteenth man to be presented to the King and Queen.

40. Private S. Harvey VC
(The Illustrated London News Picture Library)

Private S. Harvey VC of Yorks and Lancs Regiment is presented to the King and Queen. Something amusing must have occurred as everyone in the photograph is smiling or laughing.

41. Sergeant J. Smith VC
(The Illustrated London News Picture Library)

Sergeant J. Smith VC, East Kent Regiment is presented to the King and Queen in a bath chair. The conversation is focused on Smith's leg, which was likely to be the cause of his disability. Smith is pushed in his chair by a member of the Corps of Commissionaires.

The King was familiar with many of the VCs and had met some on several occasions before, not least when he actually decorated them with the VC. Despite all the names and faces the King had an excellent memory:

> "He had an amazing memory for faces" said a happy RHA bombardier[12]. "We were all put at our ease with a hearty handshake, no distinction being shown to rank. When his Majesty questioned me as to my exploit I was telling him the story and was surprised when he finished it for me".

The *Illustrated Sunday Herald* reported:

> Lieut. Michael O'Leary, dapper and proud Irishman in khaki, was engaged by the King and Queen in conversation. Their Majesties recalled that he had won his VC in 1915, and O'Leary very nearly said "Bedad and Oi did". "They called me second-lieutenant", he

---

[12] The only Royal Artillery VC present with this rank was Bombardier Isaac Lodge who won his VC on 31 March 1900 at Korn Spruit, South Africa. His VC was announced in *The London Gazette* of 26 June 1900 – exactly 20 years before the date of the Garden Party. Another representative of the Royal Artillery was present whose VC was also gazetted on 26 June 1900 – Brigadier-General E. J. Phipps-Hornby VC CB CMG.

remarked, "but begorra I've got two pips now. I've come over from Ireland specially for this, and I'm going back again. I'm happy enough there and there's no war on there at all, at all."

Another example is when the King recalled the first time he met Sergeant Oliver Brooks. The King had been thrown from his horse in France a few days before and was confined to bed; Brooks was the only VC to receive his award from the King's bedside. Brooks was awarded his VC for leading a bombing party which recaptured a section of British trench near Loos in 1915. After the war Brooks obtained employment as a commissionaire at the White Hart Hotel, opposite Windsor Castle. With his civilian greatcoat and top hat, he was a popular sight around the town. At the Garden Party Brooks wore neither his old army uniform nor his greatcoat and top hat but a suit and straw hat. *Reynolds's Newspaper*[13] reported the following comment by the King:

> "Ah, you have not your usual uniform today" remarked the King, as he cordially shook hands.

Another Windsor resident was also at the Garden Party. Sergeant Henry Engleheart, who won his VC for rescuing a sapper under heavy fire at Bloemfontein in 1900, was the Lodge-keeper at the South Western Lodge, Windsor Castle. *The Windsor, Eton & Slough Express* reported that "His Majesty had interesting chats with both the Windsor men."

Lieutenant Gabriel Coury won his VC at Guillemont on 8 August 1916. One of his daughters recalled years later that Coury had an iron handshake and at his presentation after shaking hands with the King, the King asked him to "go easy when shaking hands with the Queen."

The King and Queen engaged in a lengthy conversation with Lieutenant A. W. S. Agar VC DSO who was decorated for his attack on Russian ships in Krondstadt harbour in June 1919. A more recent VC action had also been in Krondstadt, in August 1919, when Lieutenant Gordon Steele had received the decoration, although the last VC to be gazetted was awarded to CSM George Evans on 30 January 1920 for bravery at Guillemont in July 1916. The delay between the date of the VC action and the announcement in *The London Gazette* was because the officers making the recommendation for the VC had been unable to do so as they were held as prisoners-of-war.[14]

Many VCs had previosly visited the Palace for their investitures and a select few had worked there as, for example, ADC to the King. At the time of the VC Garden Party veteran Sir Dighton Probyn VC GCB GCSI GCVO ISO had served the Royal Family, in various duties for almost 50 years.

The presentations had lasted much longer than expected as the King and Queen prolonged their conversations. The presentations began at around 4.00 pm and took more than an hour, finishing around 5.10 pm. So, on average, the King and Queen greeted five VC recipients per minute.

---

[13] Sunday 27 June 1920.

[14] Three other VCs were announced in 1920. All three were posthumous and none had been gazetted by the time of the Garden Party: one to Capt. H. J. Andrews MBE for action in Waziristan on 22 October 1919 (LG 9 September 1920), one to Lt. W. D. Kenny for action on 2 January 1920 on the North West Frontier (LG 9 September 1920) and one to Capt. G. S. Henderson DSO MC for action in Iraq on 24 July 1920 (LG 29 October 1920).

42. Lieutenant-Commander N. D. Holbrook VC shakes hands with the King
(Illustrated Sunday Herald)

Waiting to be presented is Captain J. Leach VC. Further back is Sergeant Drummer W. Kenny VC of the Gordon Highlanders in his kilt and behind him Private H. H. Robson VC of the Royal Scots wearing a bowler hat and white spats. Note the number of guests on the terrace and the waste paper basket for the used cards which the VCs gave to Major Seymour to make his announcement before the VCs were presented to the King and Queen.

9 Garden Party

After the presentations the King and Queen, along with the Royal Party, walked over to the Indian Canopy for tea, after which many of the close relatives of deceased VCs and others were presented. The Indian Canopy, with its silver supports, flanked by masses of malmaisons was reserved for the Royal Party. For others there were two large marquées with buffets of strawberries and cream and a large choice of sandwiches and cakes. The tables were decked with choice pink and crimson roses. The band of the Welsh Guards had its own awning and it played popular tunes throughout the afternoon.

According to *The Times*:

> After the presentations had all been made, refreshments were served, and many of the guests formed small parties on the lawn. Later the members of the Royal Family moved about among them, with a lack of formality which surprised some of the visitors, and some of the younger VCs were busily engaged collecting the autographs of their seniors, to be kept in memory of a wonderful afternoon.

The party was also attended by members of the Board of the Admiralty, the Army Council, the Air Ministry and prominent members of the services. Representatives from *The Times* and other newspapers were there to ensure the event was covered in the press.

43. Queen Mary speaks with an unidentified VC during the Garden Party
(The Royal Collection, © 2007 Her Majesty Queen Elizabeth II)

The Daily Telegraph reporter described the scene:

> Never was a party on these lawns so cheery, so democratic, as footmen stooped to hand ices and strawberries and cream, with delicious cakes, to small children, while parents and relatives thoroughly enjoyed the unwonted experiences. And withal, never did an assemblage show finer tact and good feeling towards their Royal host and hostess. There was no crowding round their Majesties' tea tent, no standing on chairs in mere curiosity.

One old veteran, very tired and expressing his desire for a chair, was being led about by two old ladies, doubtless well-intentioned, but far too inquisitive to find him one. When someone finally found chairs for the three of them, they lost no time in placing the old man in the middle one and either side of him continued their interrogation of the weary hero.

Mrs. Cross, wife of Corporal Arthur Cross VC told *The Daily Mirror*:

> "I shall always remember how kind everyone was to us at the Palace, and how kindly the King spoke to my husband after shaking hands with him just as you might. He expressed the kindest feelings for all the men." Of Princess Mary, she said "What I particularly noticed was that she kept very near her mother all the time".

A *Daily Mail* reporter found Sergeant Welch VC lying on the lawn smoking his pipe. His wife was feeding one of the babies from a bottle while their other child was enjoying a cream cake. Welch said it was all 'champion'. The VCs and their guests strolled across the lawns, talked with old friends and had their photographs taken. There was an air of informality which was helped by the presence of children. Some guests formed small groups, sitting on the lawn, and enjoyed the hospitality as footmen served refreshments. Cigarettes were also provided and sweets were distributed to mothers and daughters.

The Royal Artillery was well represented at the Garden Party, with 18 VCs present. One of their VC recipients reported his observations in *The Gunner*:

> Simplicity of ceremonial, homeliness, and friendly greeting - these were the features of the King's Garden Party. If the sight of small families sitting about on the grass, enjoying their tea was a somewhat unusual one, it may be doubted whether the royal hospitality was ever more appreciated, and to watch the children, with the knowledge of why they were there, was to realise the thoughtful kindliness of the host who had ruled that none were to be left behind that day.

> Grey-haired men, proud of the recognition of deeds performed long years ago and seldom talked of, looked pleased when some boy in private's uniform, or well-worn civilian clothes and cap, claimed them as fellow V.C.'s and asked them for their signatures. The rugged piper who, wounded, played his comrades up the steep side of a frontier hill, smoked his pipe in the company of a burly seaman, decorated for some gallant deed in the Great War. Here a tall young officer, his mother on his arm, talked to a companion of the stirring days, and the mother's face was good to look upon: there, the small grandson of one who gained his Cross in the far-off days of the Indian Mutiny gravely saluted the man

who had won his in the Company of the boy's uncle[15]; and older children moved about with a fuller consciousness of the scene of which they formed a part.

44. General Sir Dighton Probyn VC signs an autograph for Sergeant Issy Smith VC

This photograph was taken after the VC presentations at the foot of the West Terrace. It was published in a newspaper on 22 January 1923 the day after Probyn's ninetieth birthday. He died on 20 June 1924 aged 91. Also see photograph 36.

Before the Garden Party *The Daily Herald* had been strident in its criticism of the royal occasion but one of their reporters was mellowed by being present:

That party was wonderful. Probably it was the most thoroughly democratic gathering the Palace has ever seen. For this occasion all distinctions of rank were put aside.

Princess Mary joined the King and Queen in mingling with the VC guests. Princess Mary had been made Colonel-in-Chief of The Royal Scots (Lothian Regiment) in August 1918 and during the afternoon made a point of meeting the regiment's three VCs (see photograph 47).

---

[15] The Indian Mutiny VC was Lieutenant-General H. H. Lyster VC CB whose nephew (the grandson's uncle) was Major- General H. L. Read VC CB CMG who had won his VC as a Captain in Royal Field Artillery at Colenso on 15 December 1899. His initial L is for Lyster, named after his uncle.

A sad side to the occasion was the presence of relatives who had made the supreme sacrifice. Mrs McIver, dressed in black, wore the VC of her son, Private Hugh McIver VC MM* of The Royal Scots. She told a reporter of the *Evening Standard* that she did not know where he won his award[16] but the reverse of the cross was dated 23 August 1918. "He followed a German sentry who was on patrol, down into a dug-out and killed six men there, capturing 14", she explained.

Also present were Mr and Mrs Harris, parents of Sergeant Thomas James Harris VC MM of The Royal West Kent Regiment. They carried a portrait of their dead son in a glazed case with the VC on one side of the portrait and the MM on the other. In gold letters underneath the portrait was a description of the deed for which he was awarded the VC. The framed portrait and glazed case had been given to the couple by the firm for which Sergeant Harris had worked before the war. Mr Harris apologised for not wearing his son's VC. He said: "It is in the case and we should not like to disturb it."

45. The sons of Cpl Thomas Woodcock VC and Pte William Young VC
(Illustrated Sunday Herald)

Thomas Woodcock served in the Irish Guards, won his VC on 12/13 September 1917 near Broenbeck, Belgium but was killed at Bullecourt, France on 27 March 1918. William Young served in the East Lancashire Regiment, won his VC near Fonquevillers, France on 22 December 1915. He died of wounds on 27 August 1916 and is buried in Preston, Lancashire.

---

[16] The location was east of Courcelle-le-Compte, France. McIver's citation said he captured 20 prisoners. He was killed in action ten days later.

The Daily Despatch reported:

> Some of the fathers, mothers and wives walked alone, sadly but proudly, with the VC of some dead hero pinned on the smart gown or the rusty black mantle. Private J. Lynn, who not only received the VC but the DCM and the Cross of St. George, was represented by the girl whom he was to have married, a quiet, pathetic figure among those family reunions.
>
> Mrs. Bissett Smith was there, wearing the VC awarded posthumously to her husband, who had fought his merchantman, the *Otaki*, off Cape Race, until his last gun was silenced, and went down with his flag flying[17] "An action", King George told her, "which has never been surpassed in our glorious naval history". "It's a great thing to have this", she said, touching the bronze cross, "but this is a little thing compared with the man himself. Still, it will always be a great comfort."
>
> "Back in my old job as a carter. Yes, and forgotten all about this", said one of these gentle heroes in tweed suits. "War isn't life. It's only an interruption. Perhaps I feel that way", he apologised, confused at his expedition into philosophy, "because I'm not a soldier. I only did a bit of fighting."

The Daily News was one of the newspapers which continued to stress the social depravation of some of the VCs present. One of their reporters spoke with some VCs during the Garden Party:

> The ceremony over, the King, the Queen and Princess Mary moved among the relatives conversing with them. While they were doing so I talked with several of the VCs and heard many tales to parallel the cases of hardship cited in *The Daily News* last week. One VC told me he had to borrow a suit; another said he had to thank *The Daily News* because it was directly the result of their revelations that he had obtained his. Another said that while he had not borrowed his, he had to pinch himself in order to obtain it. "This is what my VC brought me", said a Lancashire man bitterly. "My portrait was painted at a cost of £130 and hung in the Town Hall of my birthplace[18]. I was given a gold watch and chain valued at £50. What use is that to me, and yet I can't, in decency, sell it? And to top it all, I, along with a number of other ex-servicemen, received a summons for rates incurred while I was at the war, amounting to £12. My case was the only one mentioned in the papers. The Colonel of my battalion saw it, and wrote offering to pay £7 of it outright and give the rest of the money on loan."

---

[17] T/Lieutenant Archibald Bissett Smith VC RNR engaged a raider in the Atlantic on 10 March 1917 and refused to surrender. He ordered his crew to abandon ship but chose to go down with his vessel. His VC was announced in the LG on 24 May 1919.

[18] The Lancashire recipient was Thomas Whitham VC, Coldstream Guards. Whitham, born near Burnley, had a traumatic period after the war and died in poverty, aged 36, in 1924. His VC and the portrait are on display at Towneley Hall Art Gallery and Museum, Burnley.

46. Mrs. Lucy Boughey and her son *(Illustrated Sunday Herald)*

This photograph shows the mother and brother of Second Lieutenant S. H. P. Boughey VC, 1/4th Bn. The Royal Scots Fusiliers who was killed winning his VC in December 1917 at El Burf, Palestine. He was aged 21. At the time of his death his mother told a reporter: "It was better to have died a hero than lived a coward."

The mother of Lieutenant Alfred Victor Smith VC, wore her dead son's VC as did Mrs Wignall whose son Rifleman William Mariner[19] VC of the KRRC who won his VC in 1915 but was killed on 1 July 1916. The parents of Sergeant John Meikle VC MM of the Seaforth Highlanders were present and proudly wore their son's decorations. Children of deceased VC recipients, William Young and John Woodcock, wore their fathers' VCs and their photographs appeared in newspapers the following morning. (see photograph 45) Photographs were also included in *The Daily News* of Mrs McIver, Mrs Mariner, Mrs Stubbs and Mrs Cross who was provided with a pair of boots by one of the newspaper's readers so she could go to the Garden Party.

The Daily News continued:

> Wives with domestic calculation deep set in their eyes spoke reluctantly of scraping together before they could afford this day's treat. Lastly, I met a VC who told me that some of the guests were so dissatisfied with their social conditions that they had that morning talked of drawing up a petition to the King. But feeling that it would have been out of place, they had restrained.

---

[19] Mariner changed his name before joining the army.

**47. Princess Mary meets VCs of The Royal Scots (Lothian Regiment)
during the Garden Party**
(The Royal Collection © 2007 Her Majesty Queen Elizabeth II)

Left to right : Captain J. M. Craig VC (Royal Scots Fusiliers), Princess Mary, Sergeant R. E. Elcock VC MM, Captain H. Reynolds VC MC, Private H. H. Robson VC all of The Royal Scots (Lothian Regiment), of which Princess Mary was Colonel-in Chief. The VC and medal groups of Elcock, Reynolds and Robson are on display at the Royal Scots Regimental Museum, Edinburgh Castle. Note the children in white dresses in the background.

Princess Mary

Princess Mary, the only daughter of King George V and Queen Mary, helped to organise a fund to ensure that each soldier serving on the Western Front at Christmas 1914 received a small brass tin containing cigarettes, tobacco and chocolate. The tin was embossed with her silhouette in a garland circle, the names of the Allies and *Impericum Britannicum* around the edges, and included a Christmas card and her portrait.

In July 1922 Princess Mary was married to a Yorkshire landowner fifteen years her senior: Viscount Lascelles, heir to the fifth Earl of Harewood. Their marriage was the first royal wedding to be broadcast. In 1932 the King created his daughter Princess Royal. She died in 1965.

The King and Queen talked freely with the guests as they walked slowly towards the Palace. There were six babes in arms and their fathers gently manoeuvred their wives into a position where they would meet the King and Queen. The Queen made a point of speaking with each of the mothers and enquired after their children. One example is in photograph 48 which shows Queen Mary speaking with the wife and child of Driver Frederick Luke VC.

48. Queen Mary strokes the cheek of the baby son of Driver F. Luke VC during the Garden Party *(The Daily Mirror)*

Queen Mary speaking with Jenny Luke (née Husband), the wife of Driver F. Luke VC. The couple married in April 1919 and their first child pictured here is William Husband Luke, born on 5 February 1920 in Glasgow. In the lower right of the picture is the arm and hand of a naval Captain with hand on sword holding gloves and the marching order. Note the ring worn on the little finger. There were six VCs of this rank at the Garden Party but this is probably Captain G. Campbell VC DSO** RN as he was wearing a ring on this finger (see photograph 52) and his parents were presented to the Queen on the lawn as described in Chapter 11. See photograph 53.

Driver Frederick Luke VC

Frederick Luke earned his VC on 26 August 1914 for his part, with Captain R. Reynolds and Driver J. H. C. Drain, in saving the guns at Le Cateau. His VC was announced in *The London Gazette* of 25 November 1914.

Luke later recalled that when he and Drain were in trenches near Béthune on 1 December 1914, a field officer told them that King George V wished to meet them. They were hurriedly sent to the King's inspection parade at the Locon where His Majesty invested each of them with the VC. The King advised Luke not to lose his VC in the mud but to ask his CO to send it home for safe keeping. At the 1920 Garden Party the King remembered Luke and recalled the incident.

Luke was married in April 1919. He and his wife had three sons and a daughter (his wife and first child can be seen in photograph 48). In the Second World War Luke served in the RAF Regiment as a ground gunner. He died in March 1983, aged 87, having been a VC holder for over 68 years. Luke's VC and medal group were sold later that year for £12,450.

49. The reverse of Driver F. Luke's VC
(London Stamp Exchange)

The Manchester Guardian recorded:

There was a great deal of personal and regimental pride among the crowd. Friends and relatives of the VCs were there and their comrades from battlefields and oceans many of whom themselves well deserved cheers. For instance, at the end of the day when Captain Nasmith left the Palace, trying to look inconspicuous, a young man approached him respectfully, "May I shake hands with you, sir?" The request was repeated thrice before the captain, who could better tackle the perils of Marmora better than he could face the plaudits of the crowd, turned to recognise in the speaker one of his right-hand men who had served with him through four adventurous years.

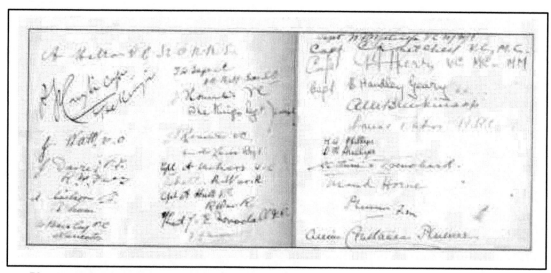

50. Autograph book used on 26 June 1920 *(Dix Noonan Webb)*

Two pages from an autograph book used to collect autographs on 26 June 1920. VCs who signed the left hand page were: E. Cooper, J. Watt, J. Davies, A. Wilcox, W. Beesley, T.H. Sage, J. T. Counter, J. Readitt, A. Vickers, A. Hutt, J. E. Woodall and T. G. Turrall. The album contains 48 VC signatures but not all were present on 26 June 1920. At the top of the page is the signature of A. Halton VC who did not attend the Garden Party but did attend the 1929 VC Dinner.

On the right hand page are the signatures of W. H. Metcalfe, C. N. Mitchell and G. F. Kerr – all Canadian VC recipients who did not attend the 1920 Garden Party but did attend the VC Dinner on 9 November 1929. Kerr died on 8 December 1929 and it is assumed their signatures were added around the time of the Dinner. It is thought this autograph book may have belonged to E. H. Geary VC who was living in Canada and attended both the 1920 Garden Party and the 1929 VC Dinner. His signature is on this page. The other signatures are not VC recipients but are likely to have been collected at the 1920 Garden Party. They include Katherine Trenchard, wife of Lord Trenchard, Field Marshal Plumer and his wife Annie Constance Plumer. The two Phillips' signatures may have been relatives of R. E. Phillips VC who was present at the Garden Party and whose signature appears on another page of the album.

Further evidence that the album belonged to Geary is that one of the VC signatories not present on 26 June 1920 was Captain D. L. Belcher VC who sat next to Geary at the 1929 VC Dinner.

This album was auctioned on 22 September 2006 by Dix Noonan Webb of London.

It was after 6.00 pm before the gathering started to break up. The Royal Party returned to the Palace while the VCs and their guests gradually departed by the North Gate where crowds were still lingering. The heroes had to pass through a double line of cheers, handshakes and waving handkerchiefs. Taxis were stopped by persistent autograph hunters, who refused to move until each VC recipient had added his name to their collection. At this point the cars supplied by the RAF returned to collect the aged and infirm VC recipients.

Edgar Rowan was a *Daily Chronicle* reporter who attended the Garden Party. At the end of the party Rowan interviewed an unnamed VC recipient whom he described as an "ex-private in mufti who had won the little bronze badge of courage in South Africa nearly 40 years ago". The only VC present fitting this description was Private John Doogan who was awarded his VC for gallantry at Laing's Nek, South Africa on 28 January 1881 while serving with 1st Dragoon Guards. Photograph 37 shows Doogan being presented to Queen Mary. Doogan's impressions of the event were reported in the *Daily Chronicle* of 28 June 1920:

> It wasn't as bad as I thought it would be – I mean it was so much bigger and better than I ever dreamed. I had worried about all this business, fair worried about it, wondering how I would get on, because one doesn't chat with the King and take tea with him every day of the week.

> But lor' bless yer, we was all at home and comfortable from the first – right from when I fell in a squad with generals and admirals at Wellington Barracks, and formed fours with them. There was a Colonel[20] as my right-hand man, and he says, "Hope you've remembered enough drill to pull me through"; and looking round I saw officers and men, I hadn't seen since we were at Elandsfontein and Laing's Nek in the early eighties.

> And then at the Palace it was all just right – only our own people there, and the King, who seemed to know all about us, and a lot of officers looking on who know the game – men like Haig: I'd wanted to see him. So it was easy and alright – just a little family party of Army people who understand and don't make a fuss.

51. Private J. Smith VC (left) and Cpl M. Heaviside VC at the Garden Party
(Illustrated Sunday Herald)

Private James Smith won his VC with the Border Regiment on 21 December 1914 for bringing in wounded men under fire at Rouges Bancs, France. His real name was James Alexander Glenn. Michael Heaviside of the Durham Light Infantry won his VC also for rescuing a wounded man who had been in a shell hole for four days and three nights. The rescue took place near Fountain-les-Groiselles, France on 6 May 1917.

---

[20] Doogan's right hand member at the front of Group No 2 was Colonel E. D. Brown-Singe-Hutchinson VC CB. Marching next to Doogan was Major-General Sir N. M. Smyth VC KCB.

Private John Doogan VC

Private John Doogan VC, 1st Dragoon Guards, served in the Zulu War of 1879 but was awarded the VC for gallantry in the First Anglo Boer War at Laing's Nek on 28 January 1881. Doogan was the servant of Major Brownlow. During a charge against the Boers, Brownlow's horse was shot and Doogan saw him on foot among the enemy. Though severely wounded, Doogan rode up, dismounted and pressed Major Brownlow to take his horse. In the process Doogan received another wound. Later in 1881 Doogan was discharged from the army as unfit for military service.

In gratitude Brownlow left in his will to Doogan a private pension of £20 per year which commenced when Brownlow died in 1926. Doogan enlisted as a Recruiting Sergeant in the First World War in which two of his sons were killed. After the death of his first wife Doogan remarried in 1928 but the marriage was dissolved as the new bride was already married. He died on 24 January 1940, aged 86 and bequeathed his VC group to the 1st Dragoon Guards.

While Doogan's VC and medals were on loan to the VC Centenary Exhibition of 1956 they went missing and for many years were assumed to be in a collection in the USA. However, in 1997 the Colonel of the Regiment was requested to collect two parcels from a London bank. The parcels contained Doogan's VC group and other items lent for the 1956 Exhibition. Because the regiment was serving in Malaya when the Exhibition closed they had been deposited in the bank where they remained for over 40 years.

10 Diary of a VC: Corporal T. W. H. Veale VC

On 28 June 1920 the *Daily Sketch* published a diary of the memorable event by Corporal T. W. H. Veale VC, the Devonshire Regiment, who won his VC on 20 July 1916 at High Wood on the Somme.

DIARY OF A VC
How it Felt to be One of the Guests at Buckingham Palace

PARENTS' PROUDEST DAY

"I Remember Your Affair," said the King
to the Corporal

---

by Corporal Veale, who won the VC on the Somme in 1916

It was one of my most memorable days. I came up from Dartmouth with my father and mother on Friday night, and they were the proudest people in the land when they were at the Palace. It was the first time they had seen Royalty, and they were greatly excited to find themselves among millions of people after being used to living among 7,000.

At Wellington Barracks, where we assembled, I met Major Fosse VC, of my old brigade, and he introduced me to the different staff officers. I got autographs from General Murlin VC, *(sic)* Commander Holbrook VC, Colonel Sherwood Kelly VC - in fact, I obtained about 150.

The refreshments there were laid out in real Army style, with red, white and blue flowers on the tables. The officer, who spoke on behalf of the Brigade of Guards, said it was a most rushed affair, and they had tried to do their best. But there was really everything we wanted there. Then we formed up in blocks and marched to Buckingham Palace. Thousands of people were cheering us; but I could not help noticing that some people were crying. We were happy and laughing, and I expect they were reminded of bereavements. One lady gave me a bouquet of flowers. "Good old Devon", she said "I come from Crediton".

At the Palace it seemed more like Coronation Day than an ordinary Tommies' parade. I was struck with the decorations and the abundance of everything and with the absolute freedom. Generals and privates were hobnobbing, and there was not a bit of swank.

Hobnobbing with Generals

The King shook hands with me and said: "I remember your affair. You won it at High Wood, didn't you?"

I said "Yes, sir" and he said, "High Wood was a nasty place, wasn't it?"

I again said, "Yes, sir" and then I remember that I ought to have said, "Your Majesty". But I was not the only one, for the officer next to me was just as bad.

The Queen also shook hands with me and said she hoped I was quite well. I did not feel a bit nervous.

I talked to several of the VCs. O'Leary told me he was going back to his old job in the Canadian Mounted Police.

I badly wanted to get Royal autographs for my collection, which I intend to put up for auction at Dartmouth for the Blind Soldiers' and Sailors' Fund.

A Court Official told me I could get them easily; but if I did everyone else would want them. So I did not try.

Not the Devonshire Kind

Father and mother enjoyed the strawberries and cream, but it was not anything like Devonshire cream. While Dad was enjoying himself the Queen came up and spoke to him.

"Are you a VC?" she asked him.

Dad said: "No, I'm one above that stage", meaning that he was too old. The Queen smiled, and he lifted his hat, and she passed on. He is still laughing about his reply.

I was signing autographs for half an hour after the party and had to escape in a taxi. It was a great day.

Private Theodore William Henry Veale VC

Private Veale was promoted to Corporal on the day he gained his VC for gallantry at High Wood, Somme on 20 July 1916. As a stretcher-bearer with the 8th Battalion, The Devonshire Regiment, at the fifth attempt Veale successfully rescued a wounded officer, Lieutenant Eric Savill, who was lying on an exposed position. After the war Savill was appointed Director of the Gardens, Windsor Great Park and was knighted in 1955. Savill Gardens are named after him. He died in 1980, the same year as Veale.

In later life Veale fell on hard times and sold his VC and medals. In 1973 they appeared for sale in a shop near Trafalgar Square and were purchased by his old regiment. Veale died on 6 November 1980, aged 87, and was cremated at Enfield Crematorium. A ceremony was held on 10 November 2002 in Dartmouth where a plaque to Veale was unveiled by his daughter, Theodora Grindell. The ceremony was also attended by Veale's granddaughter and relatives of Sir Eric Savill.

11 Memories of Captain G. Campbell VC DSO** RN

Captain Gordon Campbell VC DSO** RN attended the Garden Party and was accompanied by his wife and parents. He recalled this special day in his autobiography, *Number Thirteen*, published by Hodder and Stoughton in 1932:

> My old mother was of course very proud of her family and especially of her sons, whom she never stopped talking about. Her great wish was to have five minutes with the King in order to tell him exactly what she thought about me. Eventually her chance came. After the War, their Majesties invited all the VCs to a garden-party at Buckingham Palace, and each VC was allowed to take two next of kin. I arranged with my wife that I should take my parents, but my mother said, "No, your wife comes first, you must take her and your father." Well, in due course a special command came for Mother – which pleased her no end, and she told all her friends how she had got a special command of her own, whereas my wife and father were merely on my card as next of kin. Mother could talk of nothing else.

52. *Q* Ship Heroes : Captain G. Campbell VC DSO and
Lieutenant C. G. Bonner VC DSC**

Campbell (left) and Bonner (right) pictured at the Garden Party. Bonner was awarded his VC for his action on 8 August 1917 on *Q* Ship *Dunraven*, commanded by Campbell. In the same action Campbell received a second Bar to his DSO. In 1938 Campbell dedicated his book, *Abandon Ship*, "to my old friend and shipmate, Captain Charles George Bonner VC, DSC, the bravest man I ever met."

Captain Gordon Campbell VC DSO** RN and his fellow *Q* Ship VCs

Gordon Campbell was awarded the VC and three DSOs for his actions on *Q* Ships which were heavily armed but disguised merchant vessels. By allowing itself to be torpedoed or hit by gunfire, a *Q* Ship would lure the attacking *U*-boat to the surface and engage it at close range with hidden armaments. Such hazardous tactics required exceptional nerve and courage. Four men serving under Campbell also received the VC: **R. N. Stuart, W. Williams, C. G. Bonner** and **E. H. Pitcher**. Of the four, Stuart was the only one not present at the Garden Party.

Campbell was awarded his VC for action south west of Ireland on 17 February 1917 while commanding HMS *Farnborough*, restyled as mystery ship *Q5*. Campbell and his crew successfully lured *U-83* to the surface and sank it with 45 shells. In another action on 7 June 1917, aboard HMS *Pargust*, Campbell's crew successfully sank *UC-29*. Under Clause 13 of the VC warrant the crew were balloted on the award of two VCs: one for an officer and one for a seaman. The officers wanted Campbell to have the award which would have resulted in a Bar to his VC. However, Campbell dismissed this wish and the ballot went to *Pargust's* second-in-command **Lt. Ronald Stuart DSO**. The second VC was awarded to **William Williams DSM**. For this action Campbell received a Bar to his DSO.

In a prolonged action in the Bay of Biscay on 8 August 1917 Campbell, commanding the heavily armed *Dunraven*, engaged *UC-71*. For this desperate fight 41 members of the crew were decorated. The VC was awarded to *Dunraven's* First Lieutenant, **Charles Bonner** and **Petty Officer Ernest Pitcher DSM**. Campbell was awarded a second bar to his DSO and in 1918 he received the French Légion d'Honneur and the Croix de Guerre with Palm. Photograph 52 shows Campbell wearing his decorations but he was still awaiting the issue of his British War and Victory Medals for which he wears the ribbons only.

Between 1931 and 1935 Campbell was MP for Burnley. He wrote eight books including the worldwide best-seller, *My Mystery Ships* (1928) and an anecdotal and amusing autobiography, *Number Thirteen* (1932).

In the Second World War, Campbell was recalled from retirement by Winston Churchill to build a new fleet of *Q* Ships but the attempt ended in failure. Campbell retired from the Navy in 1943 because of ill health. He died in 1953.

The day at last came, a splendid summer Saturday afternoon. We all mustered in Wellington Barracks, Navy, Army, and Air Force. The VCs were fallen in according to their date of award *(sic)*, so that Admirals and bluejackets, Field-Marshals and privates were all mixed together. In the rear came the wounded, driven in Royal carriages. That great sailor, Admiral-of-the-Fleet Sir A. K. Wilson, was the Senior Officer of the Navy, so fell in at the top; then, led by the Guards Band, we marched out of the Barracks past Whitehall and down the Mall, through dense crowds. Some took off their hats in silence, some cheered, and others, thinking of their lost ones, wept. Personally, I felt ill at ease, and I am sure each VC was thinking, as indeed he always must, that for each living VC there are thousands who earned it far more, who died, the last man at the gun, or the last man on board. Then there are others who did noble things which were never witnessed, or which had occurred in great battles of such a size that individual gallant actions were looked upon as trivial.

My parents were at the gates as we passed through, accompanied by my wife and little boy David. After entering the Palace we were inspected by His Majesty and the Royal Family, and we marched by the King and Queen, who shook hands with each one of us. After that I witnessed one of the most democratic sights I suppose ever seen in the Royal Gardens. We were told that their Majesties were taking their tea, and hoped we would do ditto. Of course Tommy Atkins had brought, not only his wife or sweetheart, but also the babies who couldn't be left at home. There you saw little family picnic parties sitting on the grass thoroughly enjoying their tea – every man-jack of them appreciating the Royal kindness, and behaving as well as, if not better than, a Society garden-party. After tea, their Majesties came and mixed with us all. The Queen had a word for all the women and children, while the King spoke chiefly to the men. An Equerry came and told me that the King wished to see my parents and wife. I thought, now is Mother's chance. On being presented, she curtsied so low that I thought she would fall – then the King said:
"You must be very proud of your son, Mrs. Campbell."
Mother replied: "My sons are always ready to fight for their King and country."
I thought, this is a good beginning, but as the King turned to talk to my father, I noticed Mother for the first time in my life look a bit scared, and suddenly without any warning, and much to the astonishment of those around, she curtsied again and said to the King: "Well, I won't detain Your Majesty any longer." I imagine the King must have been a little taken aback at thus being dismissed. Mother had had the ambition she wanted, to shake hands with the King, but the general scene and occasion had been too much for her to say all she wanted to, especially as when H.M. the Queen had talked with her, they had talked as mother to mother about their sons in H.M.S. *Renown,* as my brother was Navigating Commander in the *Renown* when she took H.R.H. the Prince of Wales round the world. It was a great day in Mother's life and in mine, too.

53. Princess Mary, the Duchess of Argyll and Queen Mary greeting guests in the garden
(Illustrated Sunday Herald)

The naval officer on the right is Captain Gordon Campbell VC DSO. Note the marquée in the background.

12 Postscript

There was entertainment in the evening for those who wished to attend. Sir Oswald Stoll, Chairman and Managing Director of Stoll Picture Productions, and many London and provincial theatres, had generously given 300 theatre seats to VCs and their families for the evening production at the Alhambra. Normally children in arms were not admitted to the theatre but this rule was waived for the performance. Though some of the babies occasionally cried, neither the audience nor the players, who knew the reason of their presence, made any objection.

The production was *Johnny Jones, a Robey Salad*. During the interval Captain Robert Gee VC MC[21], on behalf of the guests, thanked Sir Oswald Stoll for entertaining them and congratulated him on the work he had done in connection with the War Seal[22] scheme for disabled men.

The momentous day, filled with joy, grief, admiration and pride was summarised by the King and Queen in their diaries, extracts of which are reproduced by kind permission of Her Majesty The Queen:

King George V's diary, 26 June 1920

"…At 4.0 we gave a garden party to all those that have won the Victoria Cross & their relations. They marched from Wellington Barracks, Horse Guards parade into the garden here, Officers & men together & they got a splendid reception from thousands of people, they were led by the Welch Guards band. I inspected them in the garden & then they filed past, their names were read out & May[23] & I shook hands with each one. They came in the order of the date they were awarded the VC. Dear old Probyn was the first to come having receiv[ed] his VC in 1858. Altogether 323 VCs were present. After tea we walked about & talked to them. All the family came & I think it was a great success…"

Queen Mary's diary, 26 June 1920

"…We gave a garden party to all the VCs who were available & each VC brought 2 relatives. We watched the arrival of the VCs from our balcony, they paraded in Bird cage walk & marched here via the Mall, 323 of them. A fine moving sight - We then went into the garden where G. inspected them after which G. & I shook hands with them all - This took well over an hour - Had tea & walked about talking to many of the men & their families - A very nice informal party."

---

[21] Captain Robert Gee VC MC began life in an orphanage and workhouse in Leicester and became a Conservative MP. He died 2 August 1960.

[22] The War Seal scheme was devised by Sir Edward Stoll to fund specially equipped living accommodation for disabled soldiers and their families. The seals were halfpenny stamps which were stuck on parcels and letters. They could be purchased at retailers such as Boots the Chemist.

[23] Queen Mary had previously been known as Princess May of Teck and the King always referred to her as 'May'.

Flight Lieutenant/Temporary Captain Ferdinand Maurice Felix West VC MC

The last man in the marching order on 26 June 1920 was Freddie West VC MC, one of three VCs of the RAF present on the day. Because of his artificial leg he may well have travelled in one of the cars for the disabled. West was the last of the VCs attending the Garden Party to die, aged 92, on 8 July 1988. He was also the last surviving British VC from the First World War.

West had transferred from the Royal Munster Fusiliers to the RFC in 1917. He was awarded his VC for gallantry in the air on 10 August 1918 but was badly wounded and his left leg was amputated. While commanding No. 4 Squadron during the 1930s, one of his pilots, Douglas Bader, lost both his legs in a flying accident. During the Second World War, West was the British air attaché in Switzerland and was effectively head of British air intelligence.

Later in the evening a bizarre incident occurred less than 25 miles away in Woking. Still wearing his VC, a crippled naval man[24], just returned from the Garden Party, collided with a woman cyclist on the main street. An argument erupted and as a crowd gathered a dispute began between Service and ex-Servicemen and the civil police. There were a number of fights and several attempts were made to rush the military police. However, due to the tact of an Inspector Kenwood and the discretion of the Sergeant in charge of the military police, peace was restored. No arrests were made but a number of names were taken.

Apart from the joining instructions and the official list of names prepared by the War Office, there were no mementos of the occasion which the VC recipients could take home. There was no commemorative medal and, unlike the 1929 VC Dinner, no official souvenir programme.

The Court Circular published in *The Times* of 28 June 1920 listed by name 310 VC recipients who attended the Garden Party. (This figure is slightly lower than the 321 who attended the 1929 reunion and the attendance rate of only 64 percent is also lower than 1929.) This list shows VCs in order of award by date of *The London Gazette* and therefore the order in which they were presented to the King and Queen. However, the order has a number of errors. The actual order of precedence by *The London Gazette* date is shown in the list in Appendix 2. In reality it is likely that the VCs were presented in the wrong order as published in both *The Times* and *The Daily Telegraph* of 28 June 1920. At the end of the list of names the Court Circular concluded:

> All the remaining recipients of the Victoria Cross also had the honour of being invited, but owing to absence from London and other causes were unavoidably prevented from obeying His Majesty's Commands.

---

[24] There were five non commissioned naval VC recipients at the Garden Party: Petty Officer G. McK. Samson VC RNR, Petty Officer E. H. Pitcher VC DSM RN, Leading Seaman W. Williams VC DSM RNR, Sergeant N. A. Finch VC RMA and Lance Corporal W. R. Parker VC RMLI. The unnamed VC recipient was probably W. R. Parker as he was the only one of the five VCs who was disabled at the time of the Garden Party.

Many newspapers, biographies and contemporary sources quote 324 as the number of VCs attending. It is likely that this number was based on those who said they would attend but 310 actually turned up on the day. Those who did attend had a most enjoyable day, but they had to wait nine years until the next reunion.

Appendix 3 contains an alphabetical list and the full details of those VC recipients who attended.

The centenary of the Victoria Cross was celebrated in 1956. There were various events and celebrations, including a VC Exhibition at Marlborough House, London from 15 June to 17 July, a thanksgiving service in Westminster Abbey on 25 June and a tea party for VC recipients in Westminster Hall the same day. The highlight of the celebrations was a parade in Hyde Park on 26 June, when HM The Queen reviewed approximately 300 VC recipients.

The Victoria Cross Association was formed the same month with HM The Queen as the Association's Patron. Brigadier The Rt. Hon. Sir John Smyth VC MC MP became the Chairman, and Sir Winston Churchill became the President. It was decided to hold biennial reunions, which would include a memorial service at St Martin-in-the-Fields, London. Membership was later extended to holders of the George Cross.

Although many VC and GC Association reunion receptions have been held at Buckingham Palace, the 1920 Garden Party remains unique in being the first VC reunion. King George V said of the occasion : "Such a gathering of brave men was never before seen in England."

Appendix 1

Marching order list as issued by the War Office

The marching order listed here was drawn up by the War Office before the march. It does not accurately reflect the list of those who actually marched or the marching order. Some VCs elected to miss the march and others, too disabled to march, travelled in cars provided by the RAF at the rear of the column. This list is a copy of that produced by The War Office for use on the day and it may contain errors. Some of the more obvious errors have been corrected by the authors. For example in Group No. 5, No 33 Corporal J. Collins is corrected to Royal Welch Fusiliers not South Wales Borderers as originally published. For those in Group 1 first names are shown but for all other groups only the initials are shown.

There are 17 VCs listed in Appendix 1 who did not actually attend on 26 June 1920. It is likely that they accepted the invitation and were included on the list but later decided not to attend. The authors have added an asterisk against the names of these VC recipients on the following list to show they did not actually attend.

These were:

Group	No	Name
1	13	Lieutenant R.N. **Stuart** VC DSO RNR
3	10	Colonel Sir E. T. **Thackeray** VC KCB
3	29	Sergeant R. **Bye** VC
4	5	Lieutenant-Colonel B.C. **Freyberg** VC CMG DSO
4	8	Private A. **Halton** VC
4	30	Major P. H. **Hansen** VC DSO MC
6	36	Private W. **Ratcliffe** VC
8	31	Private F. **Fitzpatrick** VC
8	32	Lieutenant W. D. **Bissett** VC
8	37	Corporal W. **Cosgrove** VC
8	38	Sergeant H. A. **Curtis** VC
8	42	Sergeant W. F. **Burman** VC
9	13	Captain T. J. **Crean** VC DSO
9	18	Lieutenant-Colonel J. H. **Reynolds** VC
9	31	Major J. A. **Sinton** VC
9	33	Major G. G. E. **Wylly** VC DSO
9	35	Major G. C. **Wheeler** VC

Missing from the list, who did attend, were:

Group	Name
1	Commander D. M. W. **Beak** VC DSO MC RNVR
7	Lieutenant W. E. **Boulter** VC
9	Trooper H. S. **Henderson** VC
9	Sergeant A. H. L. **Richardson** VC

Appendix 3 is a complete alphabetical listing of all VCs present on 26 June 1920.

HIS MAJESTY'S GARDEN PARTY TO RECIPIENTS

OF THE

VICTORIA CROSS, 26th JUNE, 1920.

List by Services and Regiments for march to Buckingham Palace.

GROUP No. 1

1. Admiral of the Fleet Sir Arthur Knyvet **Wilson**, G.C.B., O.M., G.C.V.O., R.N.,
2. Lieutenant-Colonel Lewis Stratford Tollemache **Halliday**, C.B., R.M.L.I.,
3. Commander Basil John Douglas **Guy**, D.S.O., R.N.,
4. Lieutenant-Commander Norman Douglas **Holbrook**, R.N.,
5. Commander Henry Peel **Ritchie**, R.N.,
6. Captain Henry Martin Eric **Nasmith**, C.B., R.N.,
7. Captain Edward **Unwin**, C.B., C.M.G., R.N.,
8. Petty Officer George McKenzie **Samson**, R.N.R.,
9. Commander Richard Bell **Davies**, D.S.O., A.F.C., R.N.,
10. Captain Hon. Edward Barry Stewart **Bingham**, O.B.E., R.N.,
11. Captain Gordon **Campbell**, D.S.O., R.N.,
12. Lance-Corporal Walter Richard **Parker**, R.M.L.I.,
13. Lieutenant Ronald Neil **Stuart**, D.S.O., R.N.R.,*
14. Leading Seaman William **Williams**, D.S.M., R.N.R.,
15. Chief Skipper Joseph **Watt**, R.N.R.,
16. Lieutenant Charles George **Bonner**, D.S.C., R.N.R.,
17. Petty Officer Ernest **Pitcher**, D.S.M., R.N.,
18. Captain Alfred Francis Blakeley **Carpenter**, R.N.,
19. Lieutenant Percy **Thompson-Deane**, R.N.V.R.,
20. Sergeant Norman Augustus **Finch**, R.M.A.,
21. Lieutenant-Commander Geoffrey Heneage **Drummond**, R.N.V.R.,
22. Lieutenant Harold **Auten**, D.S.C., R.N.R.,
23. Lieutenant Augustine Willington Shelton **Agar**, D.S.O., R.N.,
24. Lieutenant Gordon Charles **Steele**, R.N.,

GROUP No. 2

1. Private J. **Doogan**, 1st (King's) Dragoon Guards,
2. Major-General Sir N. M. **Smyth**, K.C.B., 2nd Dragoon Guards (Queen's Bays),
3. Sergeant H. W. **Engleheart**, 10th (Prince of Wales's Own Royal) Hussars,
4. Colonel E.D. **Brown-Singe-Hutchinson**, C.B., 14th (King's) Hussars,
5. Sergeant C. E. **Garforth**, 15th (The King's) Hussars,
6. Private H. G. **Crandon**, 18th (Queen Mary's Own) Royal Hussars,
7. Private T. **Byrne**, 21st (Empress of India's) Lancers,
8. Shoeing Smith C. **Hull**, 21st (Empress of India's) Lancers,
9. Lance-Corporal F. W. O. **Potts**, Berkshire Yeomanry,
10. S.S. Corporal A. E. **Ind**, Royal Artillery,
11. Sergeant J. C. **Raynes**, Royal Artillery

GROUP No. 2 - continued.

12. Brigadier-General E. J. **Phipps-Hornby**, C.B., C.M.G., Royal Artillery,
13. Captain G. T. **Dorrell**, Royal Artillery,
14. Bombardier I. **Lodge**, Royal Artillery,
15. Gunner A. **Smith**, Royal Artillery,
16. Captain T. H. B. **Maufe**, Royal Artillery,
17. Brigadier-General E. W. **Alexander**, C.B., C.M.G., Royal Artillery,
18. Second Lieutenant C. E. **Gourley**, M.M., Royal Artillery,
19. Driver J. H. C. **Drain**, Royal Artillery,
20. Sergeant W. **Gosling**, Royal Artillery,
21. Driver F. **Luke**, Royal Artillery,
22. Second Lieutenant G. E. **Nurse**, Royal Artillery,
23. Major-General H. L. **Reed**, C.B., C.M.G., Royal Artillery,
24. Gunner C. E. **Stone**, M.M., Royal Artillery,
25. Lieutenant-Colonel H. N. **Schofield**, Royal Artillery,
26. Lieutenant A. O. **Pollard**, M.C., D.C.M., Honourable Artillery Company,
27. Lieutenant R. L. **Haine**, M.C., Honourable Artillery Company,

---

GROUP No. 3

1. Sapper A. **Archibald**, Royal Engineers,
2. Lieutenant-General Sir F. J. **Aylmer**, K.C.B., Royal Engineers,
3. Major B. M. **Cloutman**, M.C., Royal Engineers,
4. Second Lieutenant J. L. **Dawson**, Royal Engineers,
5. Captain G. de C. E. **Findlay**, M.C., Royal Engineers,
6. General Sir R. C. **Hart**, K.C.B., K.C.V.O., Royal Engineers,
7. Lieutenant C. L. **Knox**, Royal Engineers,
8. Captain C. G. **Martin**, D.S.O, Royal Engineers,
9. Lieutenant-Colonel P. **Neame**, D.S.O., Royal Engineers,
10. Colonel Sir E. T. **Thackeray**, K.C.B., Royal Engineers,*
11. Lance-Corporal C. A. **Jarvis**, Royal Engineers,
12. Major A. H. S. **Waters**, D.S.O., M.C., Royal Engineers,
13. Lieutenant-Colonel J. M. C. **Colvin**, Royal Engineers,
14. Wing-Commander F. H. **Kirby**, O.B.E., D.C.M., Royal Engineers,
15. Major Viscount **Gort**, D.S.O., M.V.O., M.C., Grenadier Guards,
16. Lance-Corporal W. D. **Fuller**, Grenadier Guards,
17. Colonel J. V. **Campbell**, C.M.G., D.S.O., A.D.C., Coldstream Guards,
18. Sergeant O. **Brooks**, Coldstream Guards,
19. Corporal F. W. **Dobson**, Coldstream Guards,
20. Captain C. H. **Frisby**, Coldstream Guards,
21. Guardsman T. **Whitham**, Coldstream Guards,
22. Lance-Sergeant G. H. **Wyatt**, Coldstream Guards,
23. Lieutenant G. A. **Boyd-Rochfort**, Scots Guards,
24. Sergeant F. **McNess**, Scots Guards,
25. Lance-Sergeant H. B. **Wood**, M.M., Scots Guards,
26. Sergeant J. **McAulay**, D.C.M., Scots Guards,
27. Sergeant J. **Moyney**, Irish Guards,
28. Lieutenant M. **O'Leary**, Irish Guards,
29. Sergeant R. **Bye**, Welsh Guards,*

GROUP No. 4

1. Corporal R. E. **Elcock**, M.M., The Royal Scots (Lothian Regiment),
2. Captain H. **Reynolds**, M.C., The Royal Scots (Lothian Regiment),
3. Private H. H. **Robson**, The Royal Scots (Lothian Regiment),
4. Brigadier-General W. D. **Wright**, C.M.G., D.S.O., The Queen's (Royal West Surrey Regiment),
5. Brevet Lieutenant-Colonel B. C. **Freyberg**, C.M.G., D.S.O., The Queen's (Royal West Surrey Regiment),*
6. Colour Sergeant J. **Smith**, The Buffs (East Kent Regiment),
7. Private H. **Christian**, The King's Own (Royal Lancaster Regiment),
8. Private A. **Halton**, The King's Own (Royal Lancaster Regiment),*
9. Corporal J. **Hewitson**, The King's Own (Royal Lancaster Regiment),
10. Private J. **White**, The King's Own (Royal Lancaster Regiment),
11. Lance-Sergeant T.F. **Mayson**, The King's Own (Royal Lancaster Regiment),
12. Lance-Corporal T. **Bryan**, The Northumberland Fusiliers,
13. Second Lieutenant J. B. **Johnson**, The Northumberland Fusiliers,
14. Private E. **Sykes**, The Northumberland Fusiliers,
15. Private W. **Wood**, The Northumberland Fusiliers,
16. Private W. **Amey**, The Royal Warwickshire Regiment,
17. Private A. **Hutt**, The Royal Warwickshire Regiment,
18. Captain R. E. **Phillips**, The Royal Warwickshire Regiment,
19. Lance-Corporal A. **Vickers**, The Royal Warwickshire Regiment,
20. Sergeant J. **Molyneux**, The Royal Fusiliers (City of London Regiment),
21. Private S. F. **Godley**, The Royal Fusiliers (City of London Regiment),
22. Lance-Corporal C. G. **Robertson**, M.M., The Royal Fusiliers (City of London Regiment),
23. Captain R. **Gee**, M.C., The Royal Fusiliers (City of London Regiment),
24. Private J. T. **Counter**, The King's (Liverpool Regiment),
25. Captain D. D. **Farmer**, The King's (Liverpool Regiment),
26. Colour Sergeant H. **Hampton**, The King's (Liverpool Regiment),
27. Private A. H. **Proctor**, The King's (Liverpool Regiment),
28. Corporal W. E. **Heaton**, The King's (Liverpool Regiment),
29. Lieutenant-Colonel J. **Sherwood-Kelly**, C.M.G., D.S.O., The Norfolk Regiment,
30. Major P. H. **Hansen**, D.S.O., M.C., The Lincolnshire Regiment,*
31. 2nd Lieutenant G. **Onions**, The Devonshire Regiment,
32. Private T. W. H. **Veale**, The Devonshire Regiment,
33. Major J. E. I. **Masterson**, The Devonshire Regiment,
34. Corporal S. J. **Day**, The Suffolk Regiment,
35. Sergeant A. F. **Saunders**, The Suffolk Regiment,

GROUP No. 5

1. Private T. H. **Sage**, Prince Albert's (Somerset Light Infantry),
2. Private W. B. **Butler**, The Prince of Wales's Own (West Yorkshire Regiment),
3. Sergeant A. **Mountain**, The Prince of Wales's Own (West Yorkshire Regiment),
4. Lieutenant G. **Sanders**, M.C., The Prince of Wales's Own (West Yorkshire Regiment),
5. Sergeant W. B. **Traynor**, The Prince of Wales's Own (West Yorkshire Regiment),

GROUP No. 5 - continued.

6. Colonel C. **Mansel-Jones**, C.M.G., D.S.O., The Prince of Wales's Own (West Yorkshire Regiment),
7. Captain S. **Meekosha**, The Prince of Wales's Own (West Yorkshire Regiment),
8. Private G. W. **Chafer**, The East Yorkshire Regiment,
9. Private J. **Cunningham**, The East Yorkshire Regiment,
10. Captain T. E. **Adlam**, The Bedfordshire and Hertfordshire Regiment,
11. Private C. **Cox**, The Bedfordshire and Hertfordshire Regiment,
12. Lieutenant-Colonel C. C. **Foss**, D.S.O., The Bedfordshire and Hertfordshire Regiment,
13. Lieutenant F. W. **Hedges**, The Bedfordshire and Hertfordshire Regiment,
14. Corporal A. A. **Burt**, The Bedfordshire and Hertfordshire Regiment,
15. Lieutenant J. C. **Barrett**, The Leicestershire Regiment,
16. Corporal F. G. **Room**, The Royal Irish Regiment,
17. Private T. **Dresser**, Alexandra, Princess of Wales's Own (Yorkshire Regiment),
18. Sergeant W. **McNally**, M.M., Alexandra, Princess of Wales's Own (Yorkshire Regiment),
19. C. Sergeant-Major J. **Clarke**, The Lancashire Fusiliers,
20. Lance-Corporal J. **Halliwell**, The Lancashire Fusiliers,
21. Sergeant E. B. **Smith**, D.C.M., The Lancashire Fusiliers,
22. Sergeant A. J. **Richards**, The Lancashire Fusiliers,
23. Lieutenant J. **Grimshaw**, The Lancashire Fusiliers,
24. Private J. **Hutchinson**, The Lancashire Fusiliers,
25. Sergeant J. **Lister**, The Lancashire Fusiliers,
26. C. Sergeant-Major T. **Caldwell**, The Royal Scots Fusiliers,
27. Lieutenant J. M. **Craig**, The Royal Scots Fusiliers,
28. Private D. R. **Lauder**, The Royal Scots Fusiliers,
29. Private T. A. **Jones**, D.C.M., The Cheshire Regiment,
30. Sergeant J. **Davies**, The Royal Welch Fusiliers,
31. Private A. **Hill**, The Royal Welch Fusiliers,
32. Lance-Corporal H. **Weale**, The Royal Welch Fusiliers,
33. Corporal J. **Collins**, The Royal Welch Fusiliers,
34. Captain A. **Buchanan**, M.C., The South Wales Borderers,
35. Lieutenant-Colonel D. G. **Johnson**, D.S.O., M.C., The South Wales Borderers,
36. C. Sergeant-Major J. H. **Williams**, D.C.M., M.M., The South Wales Borderers,
37. Private J. **Williams**, The South Wales Borderers,

GROUP No. 6

1. Sergeant W. H. **Grimbaldeston**, The King's Own Scottish Borderers,
2. Piper D. **Laidlaw**, The King's Own Scottish Borderers,
3. Colour-Sergeant E. J. **Fowler**, The Cameronians (Scottish Rifles),
4. Private H. **May**, The Cameronians (Scottish Rifles),
5. Private J. **Towers**, The Cameronians (Scottish Rifles),
6. Lieutenant-Colonel D. **Burges**, D.S.O., The Gloucestershire Regiment,
7. Captain M. A. **James**, M.C., The Gloucestershire Regiment,
8. Private F. G. **Miles**, The Gloucestershire Regiment,
9. Lieutenant E. P. **Bennett**, M.C., The Worcestershire Regiment,

10.   Lieutenant J. **Crowe**, The Worcestershire Regiment,
11.   Lieutenant W. H. **James**, M.C., The Worcestershire Regiment,
12.   Lieutenant E. K. **Myles**, D.S.O., The Worcestershire Regiment,
13.   Private T. G. **Turrall**, The Worcestershire Regiment,
14.   C. Sergeant-Major S. J. **Bent**, The East Lancashire Regiment,
15.   Sergeant H. **Cator**, M.M., The East Surrey Regiment,
16.   Sergeant A. E. **Curtis**, The East Surrey Regiment,
17.   Corporal E. **Foster**, The East Surrey Regiment,
18.   Captain B. H. **Geary**, The East Surrey Regiment,
19.   Captain G. R. P. **Roupell**, The East Surrey Regiment,
20.   Band Sergeant T. E. **Rendle**, The Duke of Cornwall's Light Infantry,
21.   Major H. **Kelly**, M.C., The Duke of Wellington's (West Riding Regiment),
22.   Sergeant A. **Loosemore**, D.C.M., The Duke of Wellington's (West Riding Regiment),
23.   Private A. **Poulter**, The Duke of Wellington's (West Riding Regiment),
24.   Sergeant J. **Firth**, The Duke of Wellington's (West Riding Regiment),
25.   Lance-Corporal H. **Tandey**, D.C.M., M.M., The Duke of Wellington's (West Riding Regiment),
26.   Captain J. **Forbes-Robertson**, D.S.O., M.C., The Border Regiment,
27.   Sergeant C. E. **Spackman**, The Border Regiment,
28.   Private J. **Smith**, The Border Regiment,
29.   Sergeant E. J. **Mott**, D.C.M., The Border Regiment,
30.   Colonel J. W. **Chaplin**, C.B., The Hampshire Regiment,
31.   Private S. **Wassall**, The South Staffordshire Regiment,
32.   Private S. **Vickery**, The Dorset Regiment,
33.   Lieutenant G. G. **Coury**, The Prince of Wales's Volunteers (South Lancashire Regiment),
34.   Corporal J. T. **Davies**, The Prince of Wales's Volunteers (South Lancashire Regiment),
35.   Sergeant J. **Readitt**, The Prince of Wales's Volunteers (South Lancashire Regiment),
36.   Private W. **Ratcliffe**, The Prince of Wales's Volunteers (South Lancashire Regiment),*
37.   Major-General E. H. **Sartorius**, C.B., The Prince of Wales's Volunteers (South Lancashire Regiment),

---

GROUP No. 7

1.   Lance-Corporal W. C. **Fuller**, The Welch Regiment,
2.   Private H. W. **Lewis**, The Welch Regiment,
3.   Private T. **Edwards**, The Black Watch (Royal Highlanders),
4.   Private C. **Melvin**, The Black Watch (Royal Highlanders),
5.   Sergeant J. **Ripley**, The Black Watch (Royal Highlanders),
6.   Lieutenant-Colonel L. P. **Evans**, C.M.G., D.S.O., The Black Watch (Royal Highlanders),
7.   C. Sergeant-Major E. **Brooks**, The Oxfordshire and Buckinghamshire Light Infantry,
8.   Corporal A. **Wilcox**, The Oxfordshire and Buckinghamshire Light Infantry,
9.   Corporal W. **Bees**, The Sherwood Foresters (Nottinghamshire and Derbyshire Regiment),

10. Sergeant E. A. **Egerton**, The Sherwood Foresters (Nottinghamshire and Derbyshire Regiment),
11. Sergeant F. **Greaves**, The Sherwood Foresters (Nottinghamshire and Derbyshire Regiment),
12. Major C. E. **Hudson**, D.S.O., M.C., The Sherwood Foresters (Nottinghamshire and Derbyshire Regiment),
13. Sergeant W. H. **Johnson**, The Sherwood Foresters (Nottinghamshire and Derbyshire Regiment),
14. Sergeant J. **Upton**, The Sherwood Foresters (Nottinghamshire and Derbyshire Regiment),
15. Captain C. G. **Vickers**, The Sherwood Foresters (Nottinghamshire and Derbyshire Regiment),
16. Lieutenant A. J. **Knight**, The Sherwood Foresters (Nottinghamshire and Derbyshire Regiment),
17. Private H. **Kenny**, The Loyal North Lancashire Regiment,
18. Major A. R. **Hill-Walker**, The Northamptonshire Regiment,
19. Private J. **Osborne**, The Northamptonshire Regiment,
20. Sergeant J. **Welch**, Princess Charlotte of Wales's (Royal Berkshire Regiment),
21. Lieutenant D. J. **Dean**, The Queen's Own (Royal West Kent Regiment),
22. Sergeant L. **Calvert**, The King's Own (Yorkshire Light Infantry),
23. Lieutenant-Colonel H. **Greenwood**, D.S.O., M.C., The King's Own (Yorkshire Light Infantry),
24. Second Lieutenant W. **Edwards**, The King's Own (Yorkshire Light Infantry),
25. Sergeant J. W. **Ormsby**, The King's Own (Yorkshire Light Infantry),
26. Lieutenant F. W. **Holmes**, The King's Own (Yorkshire Light Infantry),
27. Private C. B. **Ward**, The King's Own (Yorkshire Light Infantry),
28. Sergeant H. **Whitfield**, The King's (Shropshire Light Infantry),
29. Corporal R. **Ryder**, The Duke of Cambridge's Own (Middlesex Regiment),
30. Captain A. M. **Toye**, M.C., The Duke of Cambridge's Own (Middlesex Regiment),
31. Private F. J. **Edwards**, The Duke of Cambridge's Own (Middlesex Regiment),
32. Colonel Sir P. S. **Marling**, Bart., C.B., The King's Royal Rifle Corps,
33. Colonel L. A. E. **Price-Davies**, C.M.G., D.S.O., The King's Royal Rifle Corps,
34. Rifleman A. E. **Shepherd**, The King's Royal Rifle Corps,
35. Lieutenant E. **Cooper**, The King's Royal Rifle Corps,
36. Major A. C. **Doxat**, The King's Royal Rifle Corps,
37. Lieutenant R. F. J. **Hayward**, The Duke of Edinburgh's (Wiltshire Regiment),
38. Lance-Corporal J. **Pitts**, The Manchester Regiment,
39. C. Sergeant-Major G. **Evans**, The Manchester Regiment,
40. Lance-Corporal A. **Wilkinson**, The Manchester Regiment,
41. Quarter-Master-Sergeant R. **Scott**, The Manchester Regiment,
42. Lieutenant C. H. **Coverdale**, The Manchester Regiment,
43. Captain J. **Leach**, The Manchester Regiment,
44. Sergeant J. **Hogan**, The Manchester Regiment,
45. Private E. **Stringer**, The Manchester Regiment,
46. Sergeant I. **Smith**, The Manchester Regiment,

GROUP No. 8

1. Sergeant J. **Carmichael**, The Prince of Wales's (North Staffordshire Regiment),
2. Lance-Corporal W. H. **Coltman**, D.C.M., M.M., The Prince of Wales's (North Staffordshire Regiment),

3. Private J. **Thomas**, The Prince of Wales's (North Staffordshire Regiment),
4. Private J. **Caffrey**, The York and Lancaster Regiment,
5. Sergeant J. B. **Daykins**, M.M., The York and Lancaster Regiment,
6. Private S. **Harvey**, The York and Lancaster Regiment,
7. C. Sergeant-Major T. **Kenny**, The Durham Light Infantry,
8. Private M. W. **Heaviside**, The Durham Light Infantry,
9. Lance-Corporal T. **Young**, The Durham Light Infantry,
10. Lance-Sergeant J. B. **Hamilton**, The Highland Light Infantry,
11. Sergeant D. F. **Hunter**, The Highland Light Infantry,
12. Corporal W. **Angus**, The Highland Light Infantry,
13. Private G. **Wilson**, The Highland Light Infantry,
14. Lieutenant-Colonel Hon. A. G. A. **Hore-Ruthven**, C.B., C.M.G., D.S.O., The Highland Light Infantry,
15. Lance-Sergeant R. **McBeath**, Seaforth Highlanders (Ross-shire Buffs, The Duke of Albany's),
16. Lance-Corporal W. P. **Ritchie**, Seaforth Highlanders (Ross-shire Buffs, The Duke of Albany's),
17. Sergeant T. **Steele**, Seaforth Highlanders (Ross-shire Buffs, The Duke of Albany's),
18. Piper G. **Findlater**, The Gordon Highlanders,
19. Colonel W. E. **Gordon**, C.B.E., A.D.C., The Gordon Highlanders,
20. Sergeant-Drummer W. **Kenny**, The Gordon Highlanders,
21. Private G. **McIntosh**, The Gordon Highlanders,
22. Lieutenant-Colonel W. **Robertson**, O.B.E., The Gordon Highlanders,
23. Captain A. E. **Ker**, The Gordon Highlanders,
24. Captain E. B. B. **Towse**, The Gordon Highlanders,
25. Sergeant E. **Lawson**, The Gordon Highlanders,
26. Lieutenant J. D. **Pollock**, The Queen's Own Cameron Highlanders,
27. Private R. **Tollerton**, The Queen's Own Cameron Highlanders,
28. Private T. **Hughes**, The Connaught Rangers,
29. Lance-Corporal J. **Murray**, The Connaught Rangers,
30. Private T. **Flawn**, The Connaught Rangers,
31. Private F. **Fitzpatrick**, The Connaught Rangers,*
32. Lieutenant W. D. **Bissett**, Princess Louise's (Argyll and Sutherland Highlanders),*
33. Lieutenant D. L. **Macintyre**, Princess Louise's (Argyll and Sutherland Highlanders),
34. Private M. J. **Moffat**, The Prince of Wales's Leinster Regiment (Royal Canadians),
35. Sergeant J. **O'Neill**, M.M., The Prince of Wales's Leinster Regiment (Royal Canadians),
36. C. Sergeant-Major M. **Doyle**, M.M., The Royal Munster Fusiliers,
37. Corporal W. **Cosgrove**, The Royal Munster Fusiliers,*
38. Sergeant H. A. **Curtis**, The Royal Dublin Fusiliers,*
39. Sergeant R. **Downie**, The Royal Dublin Fusiliers,
40. Sergeant J. **Ockendon**, The Royal Dublin Fusiliers,
41. Corporal W. **Beesley**, The Rifle Brigade (The Prince Consort's Own),
42. Sergeant W. F. **Burman**, The Rifle Brigade (The Prince Consort's Own),*
43. Lieutenant H. **Daniels**, M.C., The Rifle Brigade (The Prince Consort's Own),
44. Sergeant W. **Gregg**, D.C.M., M.M., The Rifle Brigade (The Prince Consort's Own),
45. Sergeant J. E. **Woodall**, The Rifle Brigade (The Prince Consort's Own),
46. Lance-Corporal E. **Durrant**, The Rifle Brigade (The Prince Consort's Own),

GROUP No. 9

1. Lieutenant W. A. **White**, Machine Gun Corps,
2. Corporal A. H. **Cross**, M.M., Machine Gun Corps,
3. Private R. E. **Cruickshank**, 14th (County of London) Battalion, The London Regiment (London Scottish),
4. Private J. A. **Christie**, 11th (County of London) Battalion, The London Regiment (Finsbury Rifles),
5. Private J. **Harvey**, 22nd (County of London) Battalion, The London Regiment (The Queen's),
6. Lieutenant-Colonel A. D. **Borton**, C.M.G., D.S.O., 22nd (County of London) Battalion, The London Regiment (The Queen's),
7. Captain G. H. **Woolley**, M.C., 9th (County of London) Battalion, The London Regiment (Queen Victoria's Rifles),
8. Major W. J. **English**, Royal Army Service Corps,
9. Major A. C. **Herring**, Royal Army Service Corps,
10. Private R. G. **Masters**, Royal Army Service Corps,
11. Lieutenant-General Sir W. **Babtie**, K.C.B., K.C.M.G., Royal Army Medical Corps,
12. Colonel H. E. M. **Douglas**, C.M.G., D.S.O., Royal Army Medical Corps,
13. Captain T. J. **Crean**, D.S.O., Royal Army Medical Corps,
14. Lieutenant-Colonel F. S. **Le Quesne**, Royal Army Medical Corps,
15. Major-General O. E. P. **Lloyd**, C.B., Royal Army Medical Corps,
16. Lieutenant G. A. **Maling**, Royal Army Medical Corps,
17. Colonel W. H. S. **Nickerson**, C.B., C.M.G., Royal Army Medical Corps,
18. Lieutenant-Colonel J. H. **Reynolds**, Royal Army Medical Corps,*
19. Corporal J. J. **Farmer**, Royal Army Medical Corps,
20. Rev. W. R. F. **Addison**, Royal Army Chaplains Department,
21. Rev. E. N. **Mellish**, M.C., Royal Army Chaplains Department,
22. Major-General Sir R. B. **Adams**, K.C.B., Indian Army,
23. Colonel G. H. **Boisragon**, Indian Army,
24. General Sir O'Moore **Creagh**, G.C.B., G.C.S.I., Indian Army,
25. Colonel J. **Crimmin**, C.B., C.I.E., Indian Army,
26. Colonel C. J. W. **Grant**, Indian Army,
27. Lieutenant-General H. H. **Lyster**, C.B., Indian Army,
28. Captain J. G. **Smyth**, M.C., Indian Army,
29. Major-General Sir C. J. **Melliss**, K.C.B., K.C.M.G., Indian Army,
30. Colonel R. K. **Ridgeway**, C.B., Indian Army,
31. Major J. A. **Sinton**, Indian Army,*
32. General Right Hon. Sir Dighton **Probyn**, G.C.B., G.C.S.I., G.C.V.O., I.S.O., Indian Army,
33. Major G. G. E. **Wylly**, D.S.O., Indian Army,*
34. Major-General W. G. **Walker**, C.B., Indian Army,
35. Major G. C. **Wheeler**, Indian Army,*
36. Captain G. T. **Lyall**, 2nd Canadian Infantry Battalion (Central Ontario Regiment),
37. Captain G. B. **McKean**, M.C., M.M., 14th Canadian Infantry Battalion (Quebec Regiment),
38. Lieutenant-Colonel J. H. **Bisdee**, O.B.E., Australian Imperial Forces,
39. Lieutenant L. **Keyzor**, Australian Imperial Forces,
40. Wing-Commander L. W. B. **Rees**, O.B.E., M.C., A.F.C., Royal Air Force,
41. Squadron-Leader G. S. M. **Insall**, M.C., Royal Air Force,
42. Flight-Lieutenant F. M. F. **West**, M.C. Royal Air Force,

Appendix 2

Order of Presentation of the VCs to the King and Queen

Notes

1. Some VC recipients changed their names. The names shown are those at 26 June 1920 not as gazetted, e.g. No. 53 Brown-Synge-Hutchinson, E. D. was gazetted as Brown, E. D.
In 1923 he changed the spelling from Brown to Browne.

2. Where VCs share a common LG date the order shown is the order given in the LG.

3. The names listed are chronological order of *The London Gazette* which differs at times to the actual order of presentation because the War Office lists had numerous errors. For example, the War Office had Halliday listed as LG date 24 June 1900 which was, in fact, the date of his VC deed. So Halliday is listed here as 51 Halliday, L.S.T. with the actual LG date of 1 January 1901.

4. The War Office omitted Beak, Boulter and May from their presentation list but all three were present at the Garden Party. Although May was not included in the War Office presentation list he was included in marching list. (Appendix 1)

VC Garden Party, 26 June 1920

Order of Presentation

Order	Name	LG Date	Order	Name	LG Date
A			49	Kirby, F. H.	5 Oct 1900
			50	Bisdee, J. H.	13 Nov 1900
1	Probyn, D. McN.	18 June 1858	51	Halliday, L. S. T.	1 Jan 1901
2	Lyster, H. H.	21 Oct. 1859	52	Guy, B. J. D.	1 Jan 1901
3	Chaplin, J. W.	13 Aug 1861	53	Mellis, C. J.	15 Jan 1901
4	Williams, J.	2 May 1879	54	Browne-Synge-	15 Jan 1901
5	Hart, R. C.	10 Jun 1879		Hutchinson, E. D.	
6	Wassall, S.	17 Jun 1879	55	Doxat, A. C.	15 Jan 1901
7	Creagh, O'M.	18 Nov 1879	56	Curtis, A. E.	15 Jan 1901
8	Flawn, T.	24 Feb 1880	57	Heaton, W. E.	18 Jan 1901
9	Ridgeway, R. K.	11 May 1880	58	Nickerson, W. H. S.	12 Feb 1901
10	Satorious, E. H.	17 May 1881	59	Douglas, H. E. M.	29 Mar 1901
11	Farmer, J. J.	17 May 1881	60	Farmer, D. D.	12 Apr 1901
12	Hill-Walker, A. R.	14 Mar 1882	61	Masterton, J. E. I.	4 Jun 1901
13	Doogan, J.	14 Mar 1882	62	Firth, J.	11 Jun 1901
14	Murray, J.	14 Mar 1882	63	Scott, R.	26 Jul 1901
15	Osborne, J.	14 Mar 1882	64	Pitts, J.	26 Jul 1901
16	Fowler, E. J.	7 Apr 1882	65	Schofield, H. N.	30 Aug 1901
17	Wilson, A. K.	21 May 1884	66	Traynor, W. B.	17 Sep 1901
18	Marling, P. S.	21 May 1884	67	English, W. J.	4 Oct 1901
19	Edwards, T.	21 May 1884	68	Hampton, H.	18 Oct 1901
20	Smith, A.	12 May 1885	69	Crandon, H. G.	18 Oct 1901
21	Crimmin, J.	17 Sept 1889	70	Durrant, A. E.	18 Oct 1901
22	Le Quesne, F. S.	29 Oct 1889	71	Price-Davies, L. A. E.	29 Nov 1901
23	Grant, C. J. W.	26 May 1891	72	Bees, W.	17 Dec 1901
24	Aylmer, F. J.	12 Jul 1892	73	Ind, A. E.	15 Aug 1902
25	Boisragon, G. H.	12 Jul 1892	74	Walker, W. G.	7 Aug 1903
26	Lloyd, O. E. P.	2 Jan 1894	75	Wright, W. D.	11 Sep 1903
27	Henderson, H. S.	7 May 1897			
28	Adams, R. B.	9 Nov 1897	**C**		
29	Colvin, J. M. C.	20 May 1898			
30	Findlater, G.	20 May 1898	76	Dorrell, G. T.	16 Nov 1914
31	Lawson, E.	20 May 1898	77	Garforth, C. E.	16 Nov 1914
32	Vickery, S.	20 May 1898	78	Jarvis, C. A.	16 Nov 1914
33	Byrne, T.	15 Nov 1898	79	Fuller, W. C.	23 Nov 1914
34	Smyth, N. M.	15 Nov 1898	80	Godley, S. F.	25 Nov 1914
35	Hore-Ruthven, A. G. A.	28 Feb 1899	81	Drain, J. H. C.	25 Nov 1914
36	Smith, J.	21 Apr 1899	82	Luke, F.	25 Nov 1914
			83	Holmes, F. W.	25 Nov 1914
			84	Wilson, G.	5 Dec 1914
B			85	Bent, S. J.	9 Dec 1914
			86	Dobson, F. W.	9 Dec 1914
37	Nurse, G. E.	2 Feb 1900	87	Holbrook, N. D.	22 Dec 1914
38	Reed, H. L.	2 Feb 1900	88	Leach, J.	22 Dec 1914
39	Babtie, W.	20 Apr 1900	89	Hogan, J.	22 Dec 1914
40	Phipps-Homby, E. J.	26 Jun 1900	90	Rendle, T. E.	11 Jan 1915
41	Lodge, I.	26 Jun 1900	91	Alexander, E. W.	18 Feb 1915
42	Towse, E. B. B.	6 Jul 1900	92	Kenny, W.	18 Feb 1915
43	Robertson, W.	20 Jul 1900	93	Robson, H. H.	18 Feb 1915
44	Mansel-Jones, C.	27 Jul 1900	94	Neame, P.	18 Feb 1915
45	Richardson, A. H. L.	14 Sep 1900	95	Smith, J.	18 Feb 1915
46	Gordon, W. E.	28 Sep 1900	96	O'Leary, M. J.	18 Feb 1915
47	Ward, C. B.	28 Sep 1900	97	Ritchie, H. P.	10 Apr 1915
48	Engleheart, H. W.	5 Oct 1900	98	Fuller, W. D.	19 Apr 1915

Order	Name	LG Date	Order	Name	LG Date
99	Martin, C. G.	19 Apr 1915	149	Veale, T. W. H.	9 Sep 1916
100	May, H.	19 Apr 1915	150	Bingham, E. B. S.	15 Sep 1916
101	Tollerton, R.	19 Apr 1915	151	Addison, W. R. F.	26 Sep 1916
102	Daniels, H.	28 Apr 1915	152	Buchanan, A.	26 Sep 1916
103	Woolley, G. H.	22 May 1915	153	Myles, E. K.	26 Sep 1916
104	Roupell, G. R. P.	23 June 1915	154	Davies, J.	26 Sep 1916
105	Nasmith, M. E.	25 Jun 1915	155	Hill, A.	26 Sep 1916
106	Smyth, J. G.	29 Jun 1915	156	Campbell, J. V.	26 Oct 1916
107	Angus, W.	29 Jun 1915	157	Coury, G. G.	26 Oct 1916
108	Ripley, J.	29 Jun 1915	158	Boulter, W. E.	26 Oct 1916
109	Upton, J.	29 Jun 1915	159	McNess, F.	26 Oct 1916
110	Unwin, E.	16 Aug 1915	160	Hughes, T.	26 Oct 1916
111	Samson, G. McK.	16 Aug 1915	161	Jones, T. A.	26 Oct 1916
112	Foss, C. C.	23 Aug 1915	162	Adlam, T. E.	25 Nov 1916
113	Smith, I.	23 Aug 1915	163	Kelly, H.	25 Nov 1916
114	Richards, A. J.	24 Aug 1915	164	Downie, R.	25 Nov 1916
115	Boyd-Rochfort, G. A.	1 Sep 1915	165	Edwards, F. J.	25 Nov 1916
116	James, W. H.	1 Sep 1915	166	Ryder, R. E.	25 Nov 1916
117	Potts, F. W. O.	1 Oct 1915	167	Lewis, H. W.	15 Dec 1916
118	Keysor, L.	15 Oct 1915	168	Bennett, E. P.	30 Dec 1916
119	Geary, B. H.	15 Oct 1915			
120	Brooks, O.	28 Oct 1915	**E**		
121	Maling, G. A.	18 Nov 1915			
122	Vickers, C. G.	18 Nov 1915	169	Cunningham, J.	13 Jan 1917
123	Raynes, J. C.	18 Nov 1915	170	Lauder, D. R.	13 Jan 1917
124	Pollock, J. D.	18 Nov 1915	171	Mott, E. J.	10 Mar 1917
125	Wyatt, G. H.	18 Nov 1915	172	Grimshaw, J. E.	15 Mar 1917
126	Harvey, S.	18 Nov 1915	173	Campbell, G.	21 Apr 1917
127	Laidlaw, D.	18 Nov 1915	174	Cox, C. A.	11 May 1917
128	Vickers, A.	18 Nov 1915	175	Phillips, R. E..	8 Jun 1917
129	Dawson, J. L.	7 Dec 1915	176	Haine, R. L	8 Jun 1917
130	Kenny, T.	7 Dec 1915	177	Pollard, A. O.	8 Jun 1917
131	Insall, G. S. M.	23 Dec 1915	178	Cator, H.	8 Jun 1917
			179	Ormsby, J. W.	8 Jun 1917
			180	Steele, T.	8 Jun 1917
D			181	Bryan, T.	8 Jun 1917
			182	Heaviside, M. W.	8 Jun 1917
132	Davies, R. B.	1 Jan 1916	183	Sykes, E.	8 Jun 1917
133	Burt, A. A.	22 Jan 1916	184	Gosling, W.	14 Jun 1917
134	Caffrey, J.	22 Jan 1916	185	Parker, W. R.	22 Jun 1917
135	Meekosha, S.	22 Jan 1916	186	Brooks, E.	27 Jun 1917
136	Hull, C.	3 Mar 1916	187	Foster, E.	27 Jun 1917
137	Christian, H.	3 Mar 1916	188	Welch, J.	27 Jun 1917
138	Saunders, A. F.	30 Mar 1916	189	Dresser, T.	27 Jun 1917
139	Kenny, H. E.	30 Mar 1916	190	White, J.	27 Jun 1917
140	Mellish, E. N.	20 Apr 1916	191	Readitt, J.	5 Jul 1917
141	Rees, L. W. B.	5 Aug 1916	192	Williams, W.	20 Jul 1917
142	Chafer, G. W.	5 Aug 1916	193	Craig, J. M.	2 Aug 1917
143	Proctor, A. H.	5 Aug 1916	194	Maufe, T. H. B.	2 Aug 1917
144	Stringer, G.	5 Aug 1916	195	Watt, J.	29 Aug 1917
145	Sanders, G.	9 Sep 1916	196	McIntosh, G. I.	6 Sep 1917
146	Hutchinson, J.	9 Sep 1916	197	Whitham, T.	6 Sep 1917
147	Ritchie, W. P.	9 Sep 1916	198	Cooper, E.	14 Sep 1917
148	Turrall, T. G.	9 Sep 1916	199	Grimbaldeston, W. H.	14 Sep 1917

Order	Name	LG Date	Order	Name	LG Date
200	Mayson, T. F.	14 Sep 1917	251	Crowe, J.	28 Jun 1918
201	Edwards, W.	14 Sep 1917	252	Gregg, W.	28 Jun 1918
202	Loosemoore, A.	14 Sep 1917	253	Woodall, J. E.	28 Jun 1918
203	Carmichael, J.	17 Oct 1917	254	Hewitson, J.	28 Jun 1918
204	Moyney, J.	17 Oct 1917	255	Beesley, W.	28 Jun 1918
205	Day, S. J.	17 Oct 1917	256	Poulter, A.	28 Jun 1918
206	Room, F. G.	17 Oct 1917	257	Hudson, C. E.	11 Jul 1918
207	Butler, W. B.	17 Oct 1917	258	Carpenter, A. F. B.	23 Jul 1918
208	Bonner, C. G.	2 Nov 1917	259	Dean, P. T.	23 Jul 1918
209	Pitcher, E. H.	2 Nov 1917	260	Finch, N. A.	23 Jul 1918
210	Reynolds, H.	8 Nov 1917	261	Halliwell, J.	25 Jul 1918
211	Knight, A. J.	8 Nov 1917	262	Drummond, G. H.	28 Aug 1918
212	Ockendon, J.	8 Nov 1917	263	Auten, H.	14 Sep 1918
213	Evans, L. P.	26 Nov 1917	264	Smith, E. B.	22 Oct 1918
214	Lister, J.	26 Nov 1917	265	Hunter, D. F.	23 Oct 1918
215	Molyneux, J.	26 Nov 1917	266	Macintyre, D. L.	26 Oct 1918
216	Egerton, E. A.	26 Nov 1917	267	West, F. M. F.	8 Nov 1918
217	Greaves, F.	26 Nov 1917	268	Beak, D. M. W.	15 Nov 1918
218	Hamilton, J. B.	26 Nov 1917	269	White, W. A.	15 Nov 1918
219	Hutt, A.	26 Nov 1917	270	Calvert, L.	15 Nov 1918
220	Melvin, C.	26 Nov 1917	271	Weale, H.	15 Nov 1918
221	Borton, A. D.	18 Dec 1917	272	Wilcox, A.	15 Nov 1918
222	Coverdale, C. H.	18 Dec 1917	273	Harvey, J.	15 Nov 1918
223	Collins, J.	18 Dec 1917	274	Gort, J. S. S. P. V.	27 Nov 1918
224	Sage, T. H.	18 Dec 1917	275	Frisby, C. H.	27 Nov 1918
			276	Wood, W.	27 Nov 1918

F

G

Order	Name	LG Date	Order	Name	LG Date
225	Sherwood-Kelly, J.	11 Jan 1918	277	Barrett, J. C.	14 Dec 1918
226	Gee, R.	11 Jan 1918	278	Burges, D.	14 Dec 1918
227	McAulay, J.	11 Jan 1918	279	Lyall, G. T.	14 Dec 1918
228	Spackman, C. E.	11 Jan 1918	280	Dean, D. J.	14 Dec 1918
229	McBeath, R.	11 Jan 1918	281	Williams, J. H.	14 Dec 1918
230	Gourley, C. E.	13 Feb 1918	282	Johnson, W. H.	14 Dec 1918
231	Shepherd, A. E.	13 Feb 1918	283	McNally, W.	14 Dec 1918
232	Thomas, J.	13 Feb 1918	284	Wood, H. B.	14 Dec 1918
233	Christie, J. A.	27 Feb 1918	285	Onions, G.	14 Dec 1918
234	Robertson, C. G.	9 Apr 1918	286	Tandy, H.	14 Dec 1918
235	Hayward, R. F. J.	24 Apr 1918	287	Greenwood, H.	26 Dec 1918
236	Toye, A. M.	8 May 1918	288	Johnson, J. B.	26 Dec 1918
237	Masters, R. G.	8 May 1918	289	O'Neill, J.	26 Dec 1918
238	Whitfield, H.	8 May 1918	290	Elcock, R. E.	26 Dec 1918
239	Forbes-Robertson, J.	22 May 1918	291	Moffat, M. J.	26 Dec 1918
240	Davies, J. T.	22 May 1918	292	Johnson, D. G.	6 Jan 1919
241	Stone, C. E.	22 May 1918	293	Caldwell, T.	6 Jan 1919
242	Counter, J. T.	22 May 1918	294	Clarke, J.	6 Jan 1919
243	Knox, C. L.	4 Jun 1918	295	Daykins, J. B.	6 Jan 1919
244	Cross, A. H.	4 Jun 1918	296	Coltman, W. H.	6 Jan 1919
245	Young, T.	4 Jun 1918	297	Archibald, A.	6 Jan 1919
246	Herring, A. C.	7 Jun 1918	298	Miles, F. G.	6 Jan 1919
247	Mountain, A.	7 Jun 1918	299	Towers, J.	6 Jan 1919
248	Cruickshank, R. E.	21 Jun 1918	300	Wilkinson, A. R.	6 Jan 1919
249	James, M. A.	28 Jun 1918	301	Cloutman, B. M.	31 Jan 1919
250	McKean, G. B.	28 Jun 1918	302	Hedges, F. W.	31 Jan 1919

Order	Name	LG Date
303	Doyle, M.	31 Jan 1919
304	Amey, W. L.	31 Jan 1919
305	Waters, A. H. S.	13 Feb 1919
306	Findlay, G. de C. E.	15 May 1919
307	Agar, A. W. S.	22 Aug 1919
308	Ker, A. E.	4 Sep 1919
309	Steele, G. C.	11 Nov 1919
310	Evans, W. J. G.	30 Jan 1920

Appendix 3

Alphabetical List of VCs who attended the 1920 Garden Party

The ranks of VC recipients on 26 June 1920 are correct to the best of our knowledge. Many of these ranks vary from those shown in Appendix 1 which was the official War Office list.

Alphabetical List of VCs who attended the 1920 Garden Party

Name	Rank on 26 June 1920	Other Awards to 26 June 1920	Rank as Gazetted	Regiment, Corps or Service at time of London Gazette	Date of London Gazette	March to Buckingham Palace Group and No.	Group in Palace Gardens	Order presented to King and Queen
Adams, R. B.	Major-General	KCB	Major (Brevet Lt.-Colonel)	Indian Army	9 Nov 1897	9 (22)	A	28
Addison, W. R. F.	Reverend		T/Chaplain to the Forces	RACD	26 Sep 1916	9 (20)	D	151
Adlam, T. E.	Captain		T/2nd Lieutenant	Beds and Herts Regiment	25 Nov 1916	5 (10)	D	162
Agar, A. W. S.	Lieutenant	DSO	Lieutenant	RN	22 Aug 1919	1 (23)	G	307
Alexander, E. W.	Brigadier-General	CB CMG	Lt.-Colonel	RFA	18 Feb 1915	2 (17)	C	91
Amey, W. L.	Lance-Corporal	MM	Lance-Corporal	Royal Warwickshire Regiment	31 Jan 1919	4 (16)	G	304
Angus, W.	Corporal		Lance-Corporal	HLI	29 Jun 1915	8 (12)	C	107
Archibald, A.	Sapper		Sapper	RE	6 Jan 1919	3 (1)	G	297
Auten, H.	Lieutenant-Commander	DSC	Lieutenant	RNR	14 Sep 1918	1 (22)	F	263
Aylmer, F. J.	Lieutenant-General	KCB	Captain	RE	12 Jul 1892	3 (2)	A	24
Babtie, W.	Lieutenant-General	KCB KCMG	Major	RAMC	20 April 1900	9 (11)	B	39
Barrett, J. C.	Lieutenant		Lieutenant	Leicestershire Regiment	14 Dec 1918	5 (15)	G	277
Beak, D. M. W.	Commander		Commander	RNVR	15 Nov 1918	See footnote 1	F	268
Bees, W.	Corporal		Private	Sherwood Foresters	17 Dec 1901	7 (9)	B	72

1. Beak was unlisted in the official marching list (Appendix 1) but actually marched in Group 1

Name	Rank on 26 June 1920	Other Awards to 26 June 1920	Rank as Gazetted	Regiment, Corps or Service at time of London Gazette	Date of London Gazette	March to Buckingham Palace Group and No.	Group in Palace Gardens	Order presented to King and Queen
Beesley, W.	Corporal		Private	Rifle Brigade	28 Jun 1918	8 (41)	F	255
Bennett, E. P.	Lieutenant	MC	Lieutenant	Worcestershire Regiment	30 Dec 1916	6 (9)	D	168
Bent, S. J.	CSM	MM	Drummer	East Lancashire Regiment	9 Dec 1914	6 (14)	C	85
Bingham, E. B. S.	Captain	OBE	Commander	RN	15 Sep 1916	1 (10)	D	150
Bisdee, J. H.	Lieutenant-Colonel	OBE	Private	AIF	13 Nov 1900	9 (38)	B	50
Boisragon, G. H.	Colonel		Lieutenant	Indian Army	12 Jul 1892	9 (23)	A	25
Bonner, C. G.	Lieutenant	DSC	Lieutenant	RN	2 Nov 1917	1 (16)	E	208
Borton, A. D.	Lieutenant-Colonel	CMG DSO	Lieutenant-Colonel	London Regiment	18 Dec 1917	9 (6)	E	221
Boulter, W. E.	Lieutenant		Sergeant	Northampton Regiment	26 Oct 1916	See footnote 2	D	158
Boyd-Rochfort, G. A.	Lieutenant		2nd Lieutenant	Scots Guards	1 Sep 1915	3 (23)	C	115
Brooks, E.	Sergeant		CSM	Ox and Bucks Light Infantry	27 Jun 1917	7 (7)	E	186
Brooks, O.	Sergeant		Lance-Sergeant	Coldstream Guards	28 Oct 1915	3 (18)	C	120
Browne-Singe-Hutchinson, E. D.	Colonel		Major	14th Hussars	15 Jan 1901	2 (4)	B	54
Bryan, T.	Lance-Corporal		Lance-Corporal	Northumberland Fusiliers	8 Jun 1917	4 (12)	E	181
Buchanan, A.	Captain	MC	Lieutenant	South Wales Borderers	26 Sep 1916	5 (34)	D	152

Name	Rank on 26 June 1920	Other Awards to 26 June 1920	Rank as Gazetted	Regiment, Corps or Service at time of London Gazette	Date of London Gazette	March to Buckingham Palace Group and No.	Group in Palace Gardens	Order presented to King and Queen
Burges, D.	Lieutenant-Colonel	DSO	Major, T/Lt.-Colonel	Gloucestershire Regiment	14 Dec 1918	6 (6)	G	278
Burt, A. A.	Corporal		Corporal	Hertfordshire Regiment	22 Jan 1916	5 (14)	D	133
Butler, W. B.	Private		Private	West Yorkshire Regiment	17 Oct 1917	5 (2)	E	207
Byrne, T.	Private		Private	21st Lancers	15 Nov 1898	2 (7)	A	33
Caffrey, J.	Private		Private	York and Lancaster Regiment	22 Jan 1916	8 (4)	D	134
Caldwell, T.	CSM		Sergeant	Royal Scots Fusiliers	6 Jan 1919	5 (26)	G	293
Calvert, L.	Sergeant	MM	Sergeant	KOYLI	15 Nov 1918	7 (22)	F	270
Campbell, G.	Captain	DSO**	Commander	RN	21 Apr 1917	1 (11)	E	173
Campbell, J. V.	Colonel	CMG DSO ADC	Major (Bt Lt. Colonel)	Coldstream Guards	26 Oct 1916	3 (17)	D	156
Carmichael, J.	Sergeant		Sergeant	North Staffordshire Regiment	17 Oct 1917	8 (1)	E	203
Carpenter, A. F. B.	Captain		Captain	RN	23 Jul 1918	1 (18)	F	258
Cator, H.	Sergeant	MM	Sergeant	East Surrey Regiment	8 Jun 1917	6 (15)	E	178
Chafer, G. W.	Private		Private	East Yorkshire Regiment	5 Aug 1916	5 (8)	D	142
Chaplin, J. W.	Colonel	CB	Ensign	67th Regiment	13 Aug 1861	6 (30)	A	3
Christian, H.	Private		Private	King's Own (Royal Lancaster) Regimenmt	3 Mar 1916	4 (7)	D	137

Name	Rank on 26 June 1920	Other Awards to 26 June 1920	Rank as Gazetted	Regiment, Corps or Service at time of London Gazette	Date of London Gazette	March to Buckingham Palace Group and No.	Group in Palace Gardens	Order presented to King and Queen
Christie, J. A.	Private		Lance-Corporal	London Regiment (Finsbury Rifles)	27 Feb 1918	9 (4)	F	233
Clarke, J.	CSM		Sergeant	Lancashire Fusiliers	6 Jan 1919	5 (19)	G	294
Cloutman, B. M.	Major	MC	Lieutenant (A/Major)	RE	31 Jan 1919	3 (3)	G	301
Collins, J.	Corporal		Corporal	Royal Welsh Fusiliers	18 Dec 1917	5 (33)	E	223
Coltman, W. H.	Lance Corporal	DCM* MM*	Lance-Corporal	North Staffordshire Regiment	6 Jan 1919	8 (2)	G	296
Colvin, J. M. C.	Lieutenant - Colonel		Lieutenant	RE	20 May 1898	3 (13)	A	29
Cooper, E.	Lieutenant		Sergeant	KRRC	14 Sep 1917	7 (35)	E	198
Counter, J. T.	Private		Private	King's (Liverpool) Regiment	22 May 1918	4 (24)	F	242
Coury, G. G.	Lieutenant		2nd Lieutenant	South Lancashire Regiment	26 Oct 1916	6 (33)	D	157
Coverdale, C. H.	Lieutenant	MM	Sergeant	Manchester Regiment	18 Dec 1917	7 (42)	E	222
Cox, C. A.	Private		Private	Bedfordshire Regiment	11 May 1917	5 (11)	E	174
Craig, J. M.	Lieutenant		2nd Lieutenant	Royal Scots Fusiliers	2 Aug 1917	5 (27)	E	193
Crandon, H. G.	Private		Private	18th Hussars	18 Oct 1901	2 (6)	B	69

Name	Rank on 26 June 1920	Other Awards to 26 June 1920	Rank as Gazetted	Regiment, Corps or Service at time of London Gazette	Date of London Gazette	March to Buckingham Palace Group and No.	Group in Palace Gardens	Order presented to King and Queen
Creagh, O'M.	General	GCB GCSI	Captain	Indian Army	18 Nov 1879	9 (24)	A	7
Crimmin, J.	Colonel	CB CIE VD	Surgeon	Indian Army	17 Sep 1889	9 (25)	A	21
Cross, A. H.	Corporal	MM	Private	Machine Gun Corps	4 Jun 1918	9 (2)	F	244
Crowe, J. J.	Lieutenant		2nd Lieutenant	Worcestershire Regiment	28 Jun 1918	6 (10)	F	251
Cruickshank, R. E.	Private		Private	London Scottish	21 Jun 1918	9 (3)	F	248
Cunningham, J.	Private		Private	East Yorkshire Regiment	13 Jan 1917	5 (9)	E	169
Curtis, A. E.	Sergeant		Private	East Surrey Regiment	15 Jan 1901	6 (16)	B	56
Daniels, H.	Lieutenant	MC	CSM	Rifle Brigade	28 Apr 1915	8 (43)	C	102
Davies, J. T.	Corporal		Corporal	South Lancashire Regiment	22 May 1918	6 (34)	F	240
Davies, J. J.	Sergeant		Corporal	Royal Welsh Fusiliers	26 Sep 1916	5 (30)	D	154
Davies, R. B.	Commander	DSO AFC	Squadron Commander	RN	1 Jan 1916	1 (9)	D	132
Dawson, J. L.	2nd Lieutenant		Corporal	RE	7 Dec 1915	3 (4)	C	129
Day, S. J.	Corporal		Corporal	East Suffolk Regiment	17 Oct 1917	4 (34)	E	205

Name	Rank on 26 June 1920	Other Awards to 26 June 1920	Rank as Gazetted	Regiment, Corps or Service at time of London Gazette	Date of London Gazette	March to Buckingham Palace Group and No.	Group in Palace Gardens	Order presented to King and Queen
Daykins, J. B.	Sergeant	MM	Corporal (A/Sergeant)	York and Lancaster Regiment	6 Jan 1919	8 (5)	G	295
Dean, D. J.	Lieutenant		Lieutenant	Royal West Kent Regiment	14 Dec 1918	7 (21)	G	280
Dean, P. T.	Lieutenant		Lieutenant	RNVR	23 Jul 1918	1 (19)	F	259
Dobson, F. W.	Corporal		Lance-Corporal	Coldstream Guards	9 Dec 1914	3 (19)	C	86
Doogan, J.	Private		Private	1st King's Dragoon Guards	14 Mar 1882	2 (1)	A	13
Dorrell, G. T.	Captain		Battery Sergeant Major	RHA	16 Nov 1914	2 (13)	C	76
Douglas, H. E. M.	Colonel	CMG DSO	Lieutenant	RAMC	29 Mar 1901	9 (12)	B	59
Downie, R.	Sergeant		Sergeant	Royal Dublin Fusiliers	25 Nov 1916	8 (39)	D	164
Doxat, A. C.	Major		Lieutenant	Imperial Yeomanry	15 Jan 1901	7 (36)	B	55
Doyle, M.	CSM	MM	CSM	Royal Munster Fusiliers	31 Jan 1919	8 (36)	G	303
Drain, J. H. C.	Driver		Driver	RFA	25 Nov 1914	2 (19)	C	81
Dresser, T.	Private		Private	Yorkshire Regiment	27 Jan 1917	5 (17)	E	189
Drummond, G. H.	Lieutenant		Lieutenant	RNVR	28 Aug 1918	1 (21)	F	262

Name	Rank on 26 June 1920	Other Awards to 26 June 1920	Rank as Gazetted	Regiment, Corps or Service at time of London Gazette	Date of London Gazette	March to Buckingham Palace Group and No.	Group in Palace Gardens	Order presented to King and Queen
Durrant, A. E.	Private		Private	Rifle Brigade	18 Oct 1901	8 (46)	B	70
Edwards, F. J.	Private		Private	Middlesex Regiment	25 Nov 1916	7 (31)	D	165
Edwards, T.	Private		Private	Black Watch	21 May 1884	7 (3)	A	19
Edwards, W.	2nd Lieutenant		Private	KOYLI	14 Sep 1917	7 (24)	E	201
Egerton, E. A.	Sergeant		Corporal	Sherwood Foresters	26 Nov 1917	7 (10)	E	216
Elcock, R. E.	Sergeant (see footnote 3)	MM	Lance-Corporal	Royal Scots	26 Dec 1918	4 (1)	G	290
Engleheart, H.	Sergeant		Sergeant	10th Hussars	5 Oct 1900	2 (3)	B	48
English, W. J.	Major		Lieutenant	RASC	4 Oct 1901	9 (8)	B	67
Evans, W. J. G.	CSM		CSM	Manchester Regiment	30 Jan 1920	7 (39)	G	310
Evans, L. P.	Lieutenant Colonel	CMG DSO*	Major	Black Watch	26 Nov 1917	7 (6)	E	213
Farmer, D. D.	Captain		Sergeant	King's (Liverpool) Regiment	12 Apr 1901	4 (25)	B	60
Farmer, J. J.	Corporal		Lance Corporal	RAMC	17 May 1881	9 (19)	A	11

3. Official list has Corporal but at Garden Party Elcock wears Sergeant's stripes (see photograph 47)

Name	Rank on 26 June 1920	Other Awards to 26 June 1920	Rank as Gazetted	Regiment, Corps or Service at time of London Gazette	Date of London Gazette	March to Buckingham Palace Group and No.	Group in Palace Gardens	Order presented to King and Queen
Finch, N. A.	Sergeant		Sergeant	RMA	23 Jul 1918	1 (20)	F	260
Findlater, G.	Piper		Piper	Gordon Highlanders	20 May 1898	8 (18)	A	30
Findlay, G. de C. E.	Captain	MC*	Captain (A/Major)	RE	15 May 1919	3 (5)	G	306
Firth, J.	Sergeant		Sergeant	Duke of Wellington's Regiment	11 Jun 1901	6 (24)	B	62
Flawn, T.	Private		Private	Connaught Rangers	24 Feb 1880	8 (30)	A	8
Forbes-Robertson, J.	Captain	DSO* MC	Captain (A/Lt Colonel)	Border Regiment	22 May 1918	6 (26)	F	239
Foss, C. C.	Lieutenant Colonel	DSO	Captain	Beds and Herts Regiment	23 Aug 1915	5 (12)	C	112
Foster, E.	Corporal		Corporal	East Surrey Regiment	27 Jan 1917	6 (17)	E	187
Fowler, E.	Colour-Sergeant		Private	Cameronians	7 Apr 1882	6 (3)	A	16
Frisby, C. H.	Captain		Lieutenant (A/Captain)	Coldstream Guards	27 Nov 1918	3 (20)	F	275
Fuller, W. D.	Lance-Corporal		Lance-Corporal	Grenadier Guards	19 Apr 1915	3 (16)	C	98
Fuller, W.	Lance-Corporal		Lance-Corporal	Welsh Regiment	23 Nov 1914	7 (1)	C	79
Garforth, C. E.	Sergeant		Corporal	15th Hussars	16 Nov 1914	2 (5)	C	77

Name	Rank on 26 June 1920	Other Awards to 26 June 1920	Rank as Gazetted	Regiment, Corps or Service at time of London Gazette	Date of London Gazette	March to Buckingham Palace Group and No.	Group in Palace Gardens	Order presented to King and Queen
Geary, B. H.	Captain		2nd Lieutenant	East Surrey Regiment	15 Oct 1915	6 (18)	C	119
Gee, R.	Captain	MC	Lieutenant	Royal Fusiliers	11 Jan 1918	4 (23)	F	226
Godley, S. F.	Private		Private	Royal Fusiliers	25 Nov 1914	4 (21)	C	80
Gordon, W. E.	Colonel	CBE ADC	Captain	Gordon Highlanders	28 Sep 1900	8 (19)	B	46
Gort, J. S. S. P. V.	Major Viscount	DSO** MVO MC	A/Lieutenant-Colonel	Grenadier Guards	27 Nov 1918	3 (15)	F	274
Gosling, W.	Sergeant		Sergeant	RA	14 Jun 1917	2 (20)	E	184
Gourley, C. E.	2nd Lieutenant	MM	Sergeant	RA	13 Feb 1918	2 (18)	F	230
Grant, C. J. W.	Colonel		Lieutenant	Indian Army	26 May 1891	9 (26)	A	23
Greaves, F.	Sergeant		Corporal	Sherwood Foresters	26 Nov 1917	7 (11)	E	217
Greenwood, H.	Lieutenant-Colonel	DSO* MC	A/Lieutenant-Colonel	KOYLI	26 Dec 1918	7 (23)	G	287
Gregg, W.	Sergeant	DCM MM	Sergeant	Rifle Brigade	28 Jun 1918	8 (44)	F	252
Grimbaldeston, W. H.	Sergeant		Sergeant	KOSB	14 Sep 1917	6 (1)	E	199
Grimshaw, J. E.	Lieutenant		Corporal	Lancashire Fusiliers	15 Mar 1917	5 (23)	E	172

Name	Rank on 26 June 1920	Other Awards to 26 June 1920	Rank as Gazetted	Regiment, Corps or Service at time of London Gazette	Date of London Gazette	March to Buckingham Palace Group and No.	Group in Palace Gardens	Order presented to King and Queen
Guy, B. J. D.	Commander	DSO	Midshipman	RN	1 Jan 1901	1 (3)	B	52
Haine, R. L.	Lieutenant		2nd Lieutenant	HAC	8 Jun 1917	2 (27)	E	176
Halliday, L. S. T.	Lieutenant-Colonel		Captain	RMLI	1 Jan 1901	1 (2)	B	51
Halliwell, J.	Lance-Corporal		Lance-Corporal	Lancashire Fusiliers	25 Jul 1918	5 (20)	F	261
Hamilton, J. B.	Lance-Sergeant		Lance-Corporal	HLI	26 Nov 1917	8 (10)	E	218
Hampton, H.	Colour Sergeant		Sergeant	King's (Liverpool) Regiment	18 Oct 1901	4 (26)	B	68
Hart, R. C.	General	KCB KCVO	Lieutenant	RE	10 Jun 1879	3 (6)	A	5
Harvey, J.	Private		Private	London Regiment	15 Nov 1918	9 (5)	F	273
Harvey, S.	Private		Private	York & Lancaster Regiment	18 Nov 1915	8 (6)	C	126
Hayward, R. F. J.	Lieutenant	MC*	Lieutenant	Wiltshire Regiment	24 Apr 1918	7 (37)	F	235
Heaton, W.	Corporal		Private	King's (Liverpool) Regiment	18 Jan 1901	4 (28)	B	57
Heaviside, M.	Private		Private	DLI	8 Jun 1917	8 (8)	E	182
Hedges, F. W.	Lieutenant		Lieutenant	Bedfordshire Regiment	31 Jan 1919	5 (13)	G	302

Name	Rank on 26 June 1920	Other Awards to 26 June 1920	Rank as Gazetted	Regiment, Corps or Service at time of London Gazette	Date of London Gazette	March to Buckingham Palace Group and No.	Group in Palace Gardens	Order presented to King and Queen
Henderson, H. S.	Trooper		Trooper	Buloways Field Force	7 May 1897	See footnote 4	A	27
Herring, A. C.	Major		2nd Lieutenant	RASC	7 Jun 1918	9 (9)	F	246
Hewitson, J.	Corporal		Lance-Corporal	King's Own Lancaster Regiment	28 Jun 1918	4 (9)	F	254
Hill, A.	Private		Private	Royal Welsh Fusiliers	26 Sep 1916	5 (31)	D	155
Hill-Walker, A. R.	Major		Lieutenant	Northamptonshire Regiment	14 Mar 1882	7 (18)	A	12
Hogan, J.	Sergeant		Sergeant	Manchester Regiment	22 Dec 1914	7 (44)	C	89
Holbrook, N. D.	Lieutenant-Commander		Lieutenant	RN	22 Dec 1914	1 (4)	C	87
Holmes, F. W.	Lieutenant		Lance-Corporal	KOYLI	25 Nov 1914	7 (26)	C	83
Hore-Ruthven, A. G. A.	Lieutenant-Colonel	CB CMG DSO	Captain	HLI	28 Feb 1899	8 (14)	A	35
Hudson, C. E.	Major	DSO* MC	Lieutenant-Colonel	Sherwood Foresters	11 Jul 1918	7 (12)	F	257
Hughes, T.	Private		Private	Connaught Rangers	26 Oct 1916	8 (28)	D	160
Hull, C.	Shoeing-Smith		Private	21st Lancers	3 Mar 1916	2 (8)	D	136
Hunter, D. F.	Sergeant		Corporal	HLI	23 Oct 1918	8 (11)	F	265

4. Henderson was unlisted in the official marching list (Appendix 1) but actually marched in Group 9

Name	Rank on 26 June 1920	Other Awards to 26 June 1920	Rank as Gazetted	Regiment, Corps or Service at time of London Gazette	Date of London Gazette	March to Buckingham Palace Group and No.	Group in Palace Gardens	Order presented to King and Queen
Hutchinson, J.	Private		Private	Lancashire Fusiliers	9 Sep 1916	5 (24)	D	146
Hutt, A.	Private		Private	Royal Warwickshire Regiment	26 Nov 1917	4 (17)	E	219
Ind, A. E.	Shoeing Smith Corporal		Shoeing Smith	RHA	15 Aug 1902	2 (10)	B	73
Insall, G. S. M.	Squadron-Leader	MC	2nd Lieutenant	RFC	23 Dec 1915	9 (41)	C	131
James, H.	Lieutenant	MC	Captain	Worcestershire Regiment	1 Sep 1915	6 (11)	C	116
James, M. A.	Captain	MC	2nd Lieutenant	Gloucestershire Regiment	28 Jun 1918	6 (7)	F	249
Jarvis, C. A.	Lance-Corporal		Lance-Corporal	RE	16 Nov 1914	3 (11)	C	78
Johnson, D. G.	Lieutenant-Colonel	DSO* MC	Captain (A/Lt-Colonel)	South Wales Borderers	6 Jan 1919	5 (35)	G	292
Johnson, J.	2nd Lieutenant		2nd Lieutenant	Northumberland Fusiliers	26 Dec 1918	4 (13)	G	288
Johnson, W. H.	Sergeant		Sergeant	Sherwood Foresters	14 Dec 1918	7 (13)	G	282
Jones, T. A.	Private	DCM	Private	Cheshire Regiment	26 Oct 1916	5 (29)	D	161
Kelly, H.	Major	MC*	2nd Lieutenant	Duke of Wellington's Regiment	25 Nov 1916	6 (21)	D	163
Kenny, H. E.	Private		Private	Loyal North Lancashire Regiment	30 Mar 1916	7 (17)	D	139

Name	Rank on 26 June 1920	Other Awards to 26 June 1920	Rank as Gazetted	Regiment, Corps or Service at time of London Gazette	Date of London Gazette	March to Buckingham Palace Group and No.	Group in Palace Gardens	Order presented to King and Queen
Kenny, T.	CSM		Private	DLI	7 Dec 1915	8 (7)	C	130
Kenny, W.	Sergeant-Drummer		Drummer	Gordon Highlanders	18 Feb 1915	8 (20)	C	92
Ker, A. E.	Captain		Lieutenant	Gordon Highlanders	4 Sep 1919	8 (23)	G	308
Keysor, L.	Lieutenant		Private	AIF	15 Oct 1915	9 (39)	C	118
Kirby, F. H.	Wing-Commander	OBE DCM	Corporal	RE	5 Oct 1900	3 (14)	B	49
Knight, A. J.	Lieutenant		Sergeant	Sherwood Foresters	8 Nov 1917	7 (16)	E	211
Knox, C. L.	Lieutenant		2nd Lieutenant	RE	4 Jun 1918	3 (7)	F	243
Laidlaw, D.	Piper		Piper	KOSB	18 Nov 1915	6 (2)	C	127
Lauder, D. R.	Private		Private	Royal Scots Fusiliers	13 Jan 1917	5 (28)	E	170
Lawson, E.	Sergeant		Private	Gordon Highlanders	20 May 1898	8 (25)	A	31
Le Quesne, F. S.	Lieutenant-Colonel		Surgeon	RAMC	29 Oct 1889	9 (14)	A	22
Leach, J.	Captain		Corporal	Manchester Regiment	22 Dec 1914	7 (43)	C	88
Lewis, H. W.	Private		Private	Welsh Regiment	15 Dec 1916	7 (2)	D	167

Name	Rank on 26 June 1920	Other Awards to 26 June 1920	Rank as Gazetted	Regiment, Corps or Service at time of London Gazette	Date of London Gazette	March to Buckingham Palace Group and No.	Group in Palace Gardens	Order presented to King and Queen
Lister, J.	Sergeant		Sergeant	Lancashire Fusiliers	26 Nov 1917	5 (25)	E	214
Lloyd, O. E. P.	Major-General	CB	Surgeon-Major	RAMC	2 Jan 1894	9 (15)	A	26
Lodge, I.	Bombardier		Gunner	RHA	26 Jun 1900	2 (14)	B	41
Loosemore, A.	Sergeant	DCM	Private	Duke of Wellington's Regiment	14 Sep 1917	6 (22)	E	202
Luke, F.	Driver		Driver	RFA	25 Nov 1914	2 (21)	C	82
Lyall, G. T.	Captain		Lieutenant	CEF	14 Dec 1918	9 (36)	G	279
Lyster, H. H.	Lieutenant-General	CB	Lieutenant	Indian Army	21 Oct 1859	9 (27)	A	2
Macintyre, D. L.	Lieutenant		Lieutenant	Argyll and Sutherland Highlanders	26 Oct 1918	8 (33)	F	266
Maling, G. A.	Lieutenant		T/Lieutenant	RAMC	18 Nov 1915	9 (16)	C	121
Mansel-Jones, C.	Colonel	CMG DSO	Captain	West Yorkshire Regiment	27 Jul 1900	5 (6)	B	44
Marling, P. S.	Colonel	Bart CB	Lieutenant	KRRC	21 May 1884	7 (32)	A	18
Martin, C. G.	Captain	DSO	Lieutenant	RE	19 Apr 1915	3 (8)	C	99
Masters, R. G.	Private		Private	RASC	8 May 1918	9 (10)	F	237

Name	Rank on 26 June 1920	Other Awards to 26 June 1920	Rank as Gazetted	Regiment, Corps or Service at time of London Gazette	Date of London Gazette	March to Buckingham Palace Group and No.	Group in Palace Gardens	Order presented to King and Queen
Masterton, J. E. I.	Major		Lieutenant	Devonshire Regiment	4 Jun 1901	4 (33)	B	61
Maufe, T. H. B.	Captain		2nd Lieutenant	RGA	2 Aug 1917	2 (16)	E	194
May, H.	Private		Private	Cameronians	19 Apr 1915	6 (4)	C	100
Mayson, T. F.	Lance-Sergeant		Lance-Sergeant	King's Own Lancashire Regiment	14 Sep 1917	4 (11)	E	200
McAulay, J.	Sergeant	DCM	Sergeant	Scots Guards	11 Jan 1918	3 (26)	F	227
McBeath, R.	Lance-Sergeant		Lance-Corporal	Seaforth Highlanders	11 Jan 1918	8 (15)	F	229
McIntosh, G. I.	Private		Private	Gordon Highlanders	6 Sep 1917	8 (21)	E	196
McKean, G. B.	Captain	MC MM	Lieutenant	CEF	28 Jun 1918	9 (37)	F	250
McNally, W.	Sergeant	MM	Sergeant	Yorkshire Regiment	14 Dec 1918	5 (18)	G	283
McNess, F.	Sergeant		Lance-Sergeant	Scots Guards	26 Oct 1916	3 (24)	D	159
Meekosha, S.	Captain		Corporal	West Yorkshire Regiment	22 Jan 1916	5 (7)	D	135
Mellish, E. N.	Reverend	MC	T/Chaplain	RACD	20 Apr 1916	9 (21)	D	140
Melliss, C. J.	Major-General	KCB KCMG	Captain	Indian Army	15 Jan 1901	9 (29)	B	53

Name	Rank on 26 June 1920	Other Awards to 26 June 1920	Rank as Gazetted	Regiment, Corps or Service at time of London Gazette	Date of London Gazette	March to Buckingham Palace Group and No.	Group in Palace Gardens	Order presented to King and Queen
Melvin, C.	Private		Private	Black Watch	26 Nov 1917	7 (4)	E	220
Miles, F. G.	Private		Private	Gloucestershire Regiment	6 Jan 1919	6 (8)	G	298
Moffatt, M.	Private		Private	Leinster Regiment	26 Dec 1918	8 (34)	G	291
Molyneux, J.	Sergeant		Sergeant	Royal Fusiliers	26 Nov 1917	4 (20)	E	215
Mott, E. J.	Sergeant	DCM	Sergeant	Border Regiment	10 Mar 1917	6 (29)	E	171
Mountain, A.	Sergeant		Sergeant	West Yorkshire Regiment	7 Jun 1918	5 (3)	F	247
Moyney, J.	Sergeant		Lance-Sergeant	Irish Guards	17 Oct 1917	3 (27)	E	204
Murray, J.	Lance-Corporal		Lance-Corporal	Connaught Rangers	14 Mar 1882	8 (29)	A	14
Myles, E. K.	Lieutenant	DSO	2nd Lieutenant	Welsh Regiment	26 Sep 1916	6 (12)	D	153
Nasmith, M. E. (see footnote 5)	Lieutenant Commander	CB	Lieutenant Commander	RN	25 Jun 1915	1 (6)	C	104
Neame, P.	Lieutenant	DSO	Lieutenant	RE	18 Feb 1915	3 (9)	C	94
Nickerson, W. H. S.	Colonel	CB CMG	Lieutenant	RAMC	12 Feb 1901	9 (17)	B	58
Nurse, G. E.	2nd Lieutenant		Corporal	RFA	2 Feb 1900	2 (22)	B	37

Name	Rank on 26 June 1920	Other Awards to 26 June 1920	Rank as Gazetted	Regiment, Corps or Service at time of London Gazette	Date of London Gazette	March to Buckingham Palace Group and No.	Group in Palace Gardens	Order presented to King and Queen
Ockenden, J.	Sergeant		Sergeant	Royal Dublin Fusiliers	8 Nov 1917	8 (40)	E	212
O'Leary, M. J.	Lieutenant		Lance-Corporal	Irish Guards	18 Feb 1915	3 (28)	C	96
O'Neill, J.	Sergeant	MM	Sergeant	Leinster Regiment	26 Dec 1918	8 (35)	G	289
Onions, G.	2nd Lieutenant		Lance-Corporal	Devonshire Regiment	14 Dec 1918	4 (31)	G	285
Ormsby, J. W.	Sergeant		Sergeant	KOYLI	8 Jun 1917	7 (25)	E	179
Osborne, J.	Private		Private	Northamptonshire Regiment	14 Mar 1882	7 (19)	A	15
Parker, W. R.	Lance-Corporal		Lance-Corporal	RMLI	22 Jun 1917	1 (12)	E	185
Phillips, R. E.	Captain		Lieutenant	Royal Warwickshire Regiment	8 Jun 1917	4 (18)	E	175
Phipps-Hornby, E. J.	Brigadier-General	CB CMG	Major	RHA	26 Jun 1900	2 (12)	B	40
Pitcher, E. H.	Petty Officer	DSM	Petty Officer	RN	2 Nov 1917	1 (17)	E	209
Pitts, J.	Lance-Corporal		Private	Manchester Regiment	26 Jul 1901	7 (38)	B	64
Pollard, A. O.	Lieutenant	MC* DCM	2nd Lieutenant	HAC	8 Jun 1917	2 (26)	E	177
Pollock, J. D.	Lieutenant		Corporal	Cameron Highlanders	18 Nov 1915	8 (26)	C	124

Name	Rank on 26 June 1920	Other Awards to 26 June 1920	Rank as Gazetted	Regiment, Corps or Service at time of London Gazette	Date of London Gazette	March to Buckingham Palace Group and No.	Group in Palace Gardens	Order presented to King and Queen
Potts, F. W. O.	Lance-Corporal		Private	1st Berkshire Yeomanry	1 Oct 1915	2 (9)	C	117
Poulter, A.	Private		Private	Duke of Wellington's Regiment	28 Jun 1918	6 (23)	F	256
Price-Davies, L. A. E.	Colonel	CMG DSO	Lieutenant	KRRC	29 Nov 1901	7 (33)	B	71
Probyn, D.	General	GCB GCSI GCVO	Captain	Indian Army	18 Jan 1858	9 (32)	A	1
Proctor, A. H.	Private		Private	King's (Liverpool) Regiment	5 Aug 1916	4 (27)	D	143
Raynes, J. C.	Sergeant		Sergeant	RFA	18 Nov 1915	2 (11)	C	123
Readitt, J.	Sergeant		Private	South Lancashire Regiment	5 Jul 1917	6 (35)	E	191
Reed, H. L.	Major-General	CB CMG	Captain	RFA	2 Feb 1900	2 (23)	E	38
Rees, L. W. B.	Wing-Commander	OBE MC AFC	Captain	RFC	5 Aug 1916	9 (40)	D	141
Rendle, T. E.	Band Sergeant		Bandsman	DCLI	11 Jan 1915	6 (20)	C	90
Reynolds, H.	Captain	MC	Captain	Royal Scots	8 Nov 1917	4 (2)	E	210
Richards, A.	Sergeant		Sergeant	Lancashire Fusiliers	24 Aug 1915	5 (22)	C	114
Richardson, A. H. L.	Sergeant		Sergeant	Lord Strathcona's Horse	14 Sep 1900	see footnote 6	B	45

Name	Rank on 26 June 1920	Other Awards to 26 June 1920	Rank as Gazetted	Regiment, Corps or Service at time of London Gazette	Date of London Gazette	March to Buckingham Palace Group and No.	Group in Palace Gardens	Order presented to King and Queen
Ridgeway, R. K.	Colonel		Captain	Indian Army	11 May 1880	9 (30)	A	9
Ripley, J.	Corporal		Sergeant	Black Watch	29 Jun 1915	7 (5)	C	108
Ritchie, H. P.	Commander		Commander	RN	10 Apr 1915	1 (5)	C	97
Ritchie, W.	Lance-Corporal		Drummer	Seaforth Highlanders	9 Sep 1916	8 (16)	D	147
Robertson, C. G.	Lance-Corporal	MM	Lance-Corporal	Royal Fusiliers	9 Apr 1918	4 (22)	F	234
Robertson, W.	Lieutenant-Colonel	OBE	Sergeant-Major	Gordon Highlanders	20 Jul 1900	8 (22)	B	43
Robson, H. H.	Private		Private	Royal Scots	18 Feb 1915	4 (3)	C	93
Room, F. G.	Corporal		Private	Royal Irish Regiment	17 Oct 1917	5 (16)	E	206
Roupell, G. R. P.	Captain		Lieutenant	East Surrey Regiment	23 Jul 1915	6 (19)	C	104
Ryder, R. E.	Corporal		Private	Middlesex Regiment	25 Nov 1916	7 (29)	D	166
Sage, T. H.	Private		Private	Somerset Light Infantry	18 Dec 1917	5 (1)	E	224
Samson, G. McK.	Petty Officer		Seaman	RN	16 Aug 1915	1 (8)	C	111
Sanders, G.	Lieutenant	MC	Corporal	West Yorkshire Regiment	9 Sep 1916	5 (4)	D	145

Name	Rank on 26 June 1920	Other Awards to 26 June 1920	Rank as Gazetted	Regiment, Corps or Service at time of London Gazette	Date of London Gazette	March to Buckingham Palace Group and No.	Group in Palace Gardens	Order presented to King and Queen
Sartorius, E. H.	Major-General	CB	Major	59th Regiment	17 May 1881	6 (37)	A	10
Saunders, A. F.	Sergeant		Sergeant	Suffolk Regiment	30 Mar 1916	4 (35)	D	138
Schofield, H. N.	Lieutenant-Colonel		Captain	RFA	30 Aug 1901	2 (25)	B	65
Scott, R.	Quartermaster Sergeant		Private	Manchester Regiment	26 Jul 1901	7 (41)	B	63
Shepherd, A. E.	Rifleman		Rifleman	KRRC	13 Feb 1918	7 (34)	F	231
Sherwood-Kelly, J.	Lieutenant-Colonel	CMG DSO	Lieutenant-Colonel	Norfolk Regiment	11 Jan 1918	4 (29)	F	225
Smith, A.	Gunner		Gunner	RA	12 May 1885	2 (15)	A	20
Smith, E.	Lance-Sergeant	DCM	Lance-Sergeant	Lancashire Fusiliers	22 Oct 1918	5 (21)	F	264
Smith, I.	Sergeant		Corporal	Manchester Regiment	23 Aug 1915	7 (46)	C	113
Smith, J.	Colour-Sergeant		Corporal	East Kent Regiment	21 Apr 1899	4 (6)	A	36
Smith, J.	Private		Private	Border Regiment	18 Feb 1915	6 (28)	C	95
Smyth, J. G.	Captain	MC	Lieutenant	Indian Army	29 Jun 1915	9 (28)	C	106
Smyth, N. M.	Major-General	KCB	Captain	2nd Dragoon Guards	15 Nov 1898	2 (2)	A	34

Name	Rank on 26 June 1920	Other Awards to 26 June 1920	Rank as Gazetted	Regiment, Corps or Service at time of London Gazette	Date of London Gazette	March to Buckingham Palace Group and No.	Group in Palace Gardens	Order presented to King and Queen
Spackman, C. E.	Sergeant		Sergeant	Border Regiment	11 Jan 1918	6 (27)	F	228
Steele, G. C.	Lieutenant		Lieutenant	RN	11 Nov 1919	1 (24)	G	309
Steele, T.	Sergeant		Sergeant	Seaforth Highlanders	8 Jun 1917	8 (17)	E	180
Stone, C. E.	Gunner	MM	Gunner	RA	22 May 1918	2 (24)	F	241
Stringer, G.	Private		Private	Manchester Regiment	5 Aug 1916	7 (45)	D	144
Sykes, E.	Private		Private	Northumberland Fusiliers	8 Jun 1917	4 (14)	E	183
Tandey, H.	Private	DCM MM	Private	Duke of Wellington's Regiment	14 Dec 1918	6 (25)	G	286
Thomas, J.	Private		Private	North Staffordshire Regiment	13 Feb 1918	8 (3)	F	232
Tollerton, R.	Private		Private	Cameron Highlanders	19 Apr 1915	8 (27)	C	101
Towers, J.	Private		Private	Cameronians	6 Jan 1919	6 (5)	G	299
Towse, E. B. B.	Captain		Captain	Gordon Highlanders	6 Jul 1900	8 (24)	B	42
Toye, A. M.	Lieutenant	MC	A/Captain	Middlesex Regiment	8 May 1918	7 (30)	F	236
Traynor, W. B.	Sergeant		Sergeant	West Yorkshire Regiment	17 Sep 1901	5 (5)	B	66

Name	Rank on 26 June 1920	Other Awards to 26 June 1920	Rank as Gazetted	Regiment, Corps or Service at time of London Gazette	Date of London Gazette	March to Buckingham Palace Group and No.	Group in Palace Gardens	Order presented to King and Queen
Turrall, T. G.	Private		Private	Worcestershire Regiment	9 Sep 1916	6 (13)	D	148
Unwin, E.	Captain	CB CMG	Commander	RN	16 Aug 1915	1 (7)	C	110
Upton, J.	Sergeant		Corporal	Sherwood Foresters	29 Jun 1915	7 (14)	C	109
Veale, T. W. H.	Private		Private	Devonshire Regiment	9 Sep 1916	4 (32)	D	149
Vickers, A.	Lance-Corporal		Private	Royal Warwickshire Regiment	18 Nov 1915	4 (19)	C	128
Vickers C. G.	Captain		2nd Lieutenant	Sherwood Foresters	18 Nov 1915	7 (15)	C	122
Vickery, S.	Private		Private	Dorset Regiment	20 May 1898	6 (32)	A	32
Walker, W. G.	Major-General	CB	Captain	Indian Army	7 Aug 1903	9 (34)	B	74
Ward, C.	Private		Private	KOYLI	28 Sep 1900	7 (27)	B	47
Wassall, S.	Private		Private	80th Regiment	17 Jun 1879	6 (31)	A	6
Walters, A. H. S.	Major	DSO MC	A/Major	RE	13 Feb 1919	3 (12)	G	305
Watt, J.	Chief Skipper		Skipper	RNR	29 Aug 1917	1 (15)	E	195
Weale, H.	Lance-Corporal		Lance-Corporal	Royal Welch Fusiliers	15 Nov 1918	5 (32)	F	271

Name	Rank on 26 June 1920	Other Awards to 26 June 1920	Rank as Gazetted	Regiment, Corps or Service at time of London Gazette	Date of London Gazette	March to Buckingham Palace Group and No.	Group in Palace Gardens	Order presented to King and Queen
Welch, J.	Lance-Corporal		Lance-Corporal	Royal Berkshire Regiment	27 Jun 1917	7 (20)	E	188
West. F. M. F.	Flight-Lieutenant	MC	A/Captain	RAF	8 Nov 1918	9 (42)	F	267
White, J.	Private		Private	King's Own Royal Lancaster Regiment	27 Jun 1917	4 (10)	E	190
White, W. A.	Lieutenant		2nd Lieutenant	Machine Gun Corps	15 Nov 1918	9 (1)	F	269
Whitfield, H.	Sergeant		Private	Shropshire Light Infantry	8 May 1918	7 (28)	F	238
Whitham, T.	Guardsman		Guardsman	Coldstream Guards	6 Sep 1917	3 (21)	E	197
Wilcox, A.	Corporal		Lance-Corporal	Ox and Bucks Light Infantry	15 Nov 1918	7 (8)	F	272
Wilkinson, A. R.	Lance-Corporal		Private	Manchester Regiment	6 Jan 1919	7 (40)	G	300
Williams, J.	Private		Private	24th Regiment	2 May 1879	5 (37)	A	4
Williams, J. H.	CSM	DCM MM*	CSM	South Wales Borderers	14 Dec 1918	5 (36)	G	281
Williams, W.	Leading Seaman	DSM*	Seaman	RNR	20 Jul 1917	1 (14)	E	192
Wilson, G.	Private		Private	HLI	5 Dec 1914	8 (13)	C	84
Wilson, A. K.	Admiral of the Fleet	GCB OM GCVO	Captain	RN	21 May 1884	1 (1)	A	17

Name	Rank on 26 June 1920	Other Awards to 26 June 1920	Rank as Gazetted	Regiment, Corps or Service at time of London Gazette	Date of London Gazette	March to Buckingham Palace Group and No.	Group in Palace Gardens	Order presented to King and Queen
Wood, H. B.	Lance-Sergeant	MM	Corporal	Scots Guards	14 Dec 1918	3 (25)	G	284
Wood, W.	Private		Private	Northumberland Fusiliers	27 Nov 1918	4 (15)	F	276
Woodall, J. E.	Sergeant		Lance-Sergeant	Rifle Brigade	28 Jun 1918	8 (45)	F	253
Woolley, G. H.	Captain	MC	2nd Lieutenant	Queen Victoria's Rifles	22 May 1915	9 (7)	C	103
Wright, W. D.	Brigadier-General	CMG DSO	Lieutenant	Royal West Surrey Regiment	11 Sep 1903	4 (4)	B	75
Wyatt, G. H.	Lance-Sergeant		Lance-Corporal	Coldstream Guards	18 Nov 1915	3 (22)	C	125
Young, T.	Lance-Corporal		Private	DLI	4 Jun 1918	8 (9)	F	245

Bibliography

Books

Bancroft, James, *The Zulu War VCs,* James Bancroft, Eccles, 1992

Batchelor, Peter F. and Matson, Christopher, *VCs of the First World War: The Western Front 1915*, Sutton Publishing, Stroud, 1997

Brown, Jane and Sykes, Christopher Simon, *The Garden at Buckingham Palace: An Illustrated History*, Royal Collection, London, 2004

Campbell, Rear Admiral, VC DSO MP, *Number Thirteen*, Hodder and Stoughton, London, 1932

Coates, Peter, *The Gardens of Buckingham Palace*, Michael Joseph, London, 1978

Cooksley, Peter G., *VCs of the First World War: The Air VCs*, Sutton Publishing, Stroud, 1996

Creagh, Sir O'Moore VC GCB GCSI and Humphris, E. M., *The VC and DSO,* Standard Art Book Co., London, 1924

Crook, M. J., *The Evolution of the Victoria Cross*, Midas Books, Tunbridge Wells, 1975

Gliddon, Gerald, *VCs of the First World War: The Somme*, Alan Sutton Publishing, Stroud, 1994

Gliddon, Gerald, *VCs of the First World War: 1914*, Alan Sutton Publishing, Stroud, 1994

Gliddon, Gerald, *VCs of the First World War: Spring Offensive 1918*, Sutton Publishing, Stroud, 1997

Gliddon, Gerald, *VCs of the First World War: Arras and Messines 1917*, Sutton Publishing, Stroud, 1998

Gliddon, Gerald, *VCs of the First World War: The Road to Victory 1918*, Sutton Publishing, Stroud, 2000

Gliddon, Gerald, *VCs of the First World War: The Final Days 1918*, Sutton Publishing, Stroud, 2000

Gliddon, Gerald, *VCs of the First World War: Cambrai 1917,* Sutton Publishing, Stroud, 2004

Gliddon, Gerald, *VCs of the First World War: The Sideshows,* Sutton Publishing, Stroud, 2005

Graeme, Bruce, *A Century of Buckingham Palace 1837-1937,* Hutchinson, London, 1937

Harvey, David, *Monuments to Courage: Victoria Cross Headstones and Memorials*, Kevin and Kay Patience, Bahrain, 1999

Hunt, Derek, *Valour Beyond All Praise: Harry Greenwood VC*, Derek Hunt, Windsor, 2003

Macleod, J. R., *Portrait of a Soldier*, Dingwall Museum Trust, Dingwall, 1992

Marling, Colonel Sir Percival, Bt VC CB, *Rifleman and Hussar,* John Murray, London, 1931

Mulholland, John and Jordan, Alan, *Victoria Cross Bibliography*, Spink, London, 1999

Nash, Roy, *Buckingham Palace: The Place and the People*, Macdonald, London, 1980

Rose, Kenneth, *King George V*, Weidenfeld and Nicholson, London, 1983

Smyth, Sir John VC MC, *Milestones*, Sidgwick and Jackson, London, 1979

Snelling, Stephen, *VCs of The First World War: Gallipoli*, Alan Sutton Publishing, Stroud, 1995

Snelling, Stephen, *VCs of The First World War: Passchendaele 1917*, Sutton Publishing, Stroud, 1998

Snelling, Stephen, *VCs of The First World War: The Naval VCs*, Sutton Publishing, Stroud, 2002

This England, *The Register of the Victoria Cross (Third Edition)*, This England Books, Cheltenham, 1997

Turner, E. S., *The Court of St. James,* Michael Joseph, London, 1959

Van der Kiste, John, *King George V's Children*, Alan Sutton Publishing, Stroud, 1991

Williams, W. Alister, *The VCs of Wales and the Welsh Regiments*, Bridge Books, Wrexham, 1984

Who Was Who

The Annual Register, 1920

Websites

The History of the Victoria Cross   www.victoriacross.org.uk/
The Victoria Cross Society   www.victoriacrosssociety.com/

Archives

Canon Lummis VC files held at the National Army Museum on behalf of the Military Historical Society

Further Reading

A number of VCs present at the Garden Party became the subject of biographies or autobiographies. Each of the VCs of the First World War have a chapter in one of Sutton's series *VCs of the First World War* (see bibliography above). For a useful reference on where to find books on the VC and individual recipients see *Victoria Cross Bibliography* by Mulholland and Jordan, Spink, London, 1999.

Newspaper Sources

Daily Express	26 June 1920
The Daily Graphic	26 June 1920
The Daily Herald	26 June 1920
The Daily Mail	26 June 1920
The Daily Mirror	26 June 1920
The Daily Telegraph	26 June 1920
Evening Standard	26 June 1920
The Manchester Guardian	26 June 1920
The Times	26 June 1920
News of the World	27 June 1920
The Observer	27 June 1920
Reynolds's Newspaper	27 June 1920
Sunday Express	27 June 1920
Sunday Pictorial	27 June 1920
The Sunday Times	27 June 1920
Illustrated Sunday Herald	27 June 1920
The Weekly Dispatch	27 June 1920
Daily Chronicle	28 June 1920
Daily Express	28 June 1920
The Daily Graphic	28 June 1920
The Daily Herald	28 June 1920
The Daily Mail	28 June 1920
The Daily Mirror	28 June 1920
The Daily News	28 June 1920
Daily Sketch	28 June 1920
The Daily Telegraph	28 June 1920
The Manchester Guardian	28 June 1920
The Morning Post	28 June 1920
The Times	28 June 1920
The Illustrated London News	3 July 1920
The Windsor, Eton and Slough Express	3 July 1920

Notes on Newspaper Sources

Since 1920 many of the above newspapers have changed titles, merged or ceased publication:

- *The Daily Graphic* merged in 1926 with the *Daily Sketch*, which in turn merged with *The Daily Mail* in 1971.
- *The Daily News* and the *Daily Chronicle* merged in 1930 to form the *News Chronicle*. This newspaper merged with *The Daily Mail* in 1960.
- *The Morning Post* merged with *The Daily Telegraph* in 1937.
- *The Manchester Guardian* changed its title to *The Guardian* in 1959.
- *Reynolds's Newspaper* became the *Sunday Citizen* in 1962 and ceased publication in 1967.
- The *Sunday Pictorial* became the *Sunday Mirror* in 1963.
- *The Daily Herald* became *The Sun* in 1964.

About the Authors

Derek Hunt, a retired bank manager, is a researcher and author with a specialist interest in the VC. He has contributed to numerous VC books and writes for several publications including the Journal of the Victoria Cross Society. In 1998 Derek organised the Windsor Victoria Cross Exhibition, honouring VC recipients connected with his hometown of Windsor. He wrote a biography of one of these VCs, *Valour Beyond All Praise – Harry Greenwood VC*, which was published in 2003.

John Mulholland is a chartered chemical engineer and a director of a large UK energy consultancy. His interest in the VC stems from his school days at Stonyhurst College whose old boys won seven VCs. John writes extensively on VC recipients, particularly in the Journal of the Victoria Cross Society. He is a member of the Orders and Medals Research Society and is a co-author of *Victoria Cross Bibliography,* published by Spink.